MW00651660

IN EXTREMIS

Are the Passengers Safe?

THE
ANDREA DORIA / STOCKHOLM
COLLISION

By
CAPTAIN ROBERT J. MEURN
MASTER MARINER

In Extremis
Are the Passengers Safe?
Copyright © 2018 by Robert Meurn

Library of Congress Control Number: 2017953496
ISBN-13:   Paperback: 978-1-64045-998-4
            PDF: 978-1-64151-000-4
            ePub: 978-1-64151-001-1
            Kindle: 978-1-64151-002-8

Printed in the United States of America

LitFire LLC
1-800-511-9787
www.litfirepublishing.com
order@litfirepublishing.com

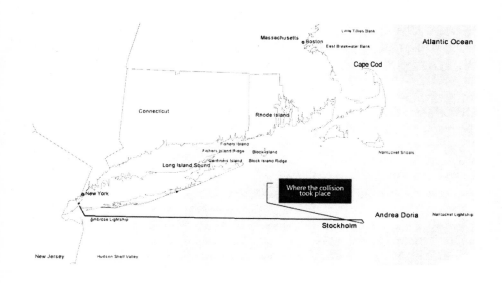

CONTENTS

INTRODUCTION

On April 9, 1972, Captain Piero Calamai passed away at the age of 75 in Genoa, Italy. Captain Calamai was Master of the *Andrea Doria* on July 25, 1956, when at 11:11 PM (2311) the *MV Stockholm* impaled her ice-reinforced bow into the starboard side of his vessel. The collision resulted in the deaths of 44 passengers aboard the *Andrea Doria*, but 1,662 souls survived and were saved. Captain Calamai was so shattered by the tragedy that he abandoned the sea and went into permanent seclusion. After the disaster the Captain was quoted, *"When I was a boy all my life I loved the sea; now I hate it."* Friends said he died of *"crepacuore"* – a broken heart. His last words before he died were, *"Are the passengers safe?"*

As a deck cadet aboard the *SS Excambion* enroute to New York during the night of July 25, 1956, we were surrounded by a thick opaque fog. The *Excambion* was on stand -by engines at a slow speed when the SOS Auto Alarm sounded. Our ship was too far south to render assistance but the news caused a rush to judgment as to blame. As a Swedish American, whose father was born in *Stockholm* and a grandfather who was a Captain in the Swedish Merchant Marine, I, of course, believed the *Stockholm* was not at fault and the book <u>Collision Course</u> by Alvin Moscow published in 1959 confirmed my opinion.

During a training ship cruise aboard the *TS Empire State* in 1970, I first met John Carrothers who had a theory on why the *Andrea Doria* and *Stockholm* collided. His theory seemed plausible but I did not become an advocate until I did my own research on the ship bridge simulator at the U.S. Merchant Marine Academy in 1993.

John was a compassionate man who truly cared by his fellow man and those in his profession. In 1956 when Captain Calamai appeared to become the scapegoat for this radar-assisted collision, John was the only man who came to his defense. His articles in the <u>U.S. Naval Institute Proceedings</u> defended Captain Calamai from the injustice of the inquiry findings and the inferences of books about the collision. An excerpt from his letter to Captain Calamai on March 12, 1972 stated: *"It now pleases me to send a copy of the United States Naval Institute Proceedings, from our Naval Academy at Annapolis, in which the Stockholm's error is explained. During all these years I have intentionally refrained from contacting you as I did not want to aggravate the terrible wound that still must be in your heart. Now that the start has been made we fully intend to follow the matter through to its proper conclusion. This will not only exonerate you but will also serve those interested in safety and education. Incidentally, the article is now being used for educational purposes in some and perhaps all of our maritime and naval academies.*

In the meantime, it may be some satisfaction to you to know that those of us who watched you suffer through the disgraceful official inquiry in New York have nothing but sympathy, admiration and respect for you. Sympathy because of the brutal treatment you were subjected to in the Federal Court of the United States, admiration for your absolute integrity and loyalty to your owners and respect for the manner in which you conducted yourself since the accident.

Rest assured Captain Calamai, there are many of us who would be more than willing to serve under your command at any time. Most sincerely, John C. Carrothers"

This letter along with the article was found unopened when Captain Calamai died one month later. His daughters stated that their father died without knowing of John Carrother's attempt to explain the truth of the collision and to clear his name.

Unfortunately, the accident was never thoroughly investigated and controversy remains today fueled by many books and articles that are not supported by facts. Bias and prejudice formulate many opinions.

What follows is a factual account of what really happened on that foggy night of July 25, 1956.

DEDICATIONS

In memory of Captain Piero Calamai (1898-1972)

To John C. Carrothers (1904-1991)

A shipmate and friend in appreciation of his
contributions to Safety of Life at Sea

Dedicated in affectionate remembrance of
David A. Bright (1957-2006)

For his relentless search for the truth and
devotion to the *Andrea Doria* legacy

Captain Piero Calamai

John C. Carrothers

David Bright showing Captain Badano memorabilia recovered from the Andrea
Doria in July, 1996 at 40th reunion of the survivors

ACKNOWLEDGEMENTS

F irst and foremost, I must acknowledge John C. Carrothers, who I first met in 1970. He soon convinced me that the cause of the collision was the misuse of the radar by the *Stockholm's* third officer of the watch, Ernst Carstens-Johanssen.

John C. Carrothers devoted most of his life pursuing justice. Although the majority of his pursuits were maritime related, he was never hesitant to speak the truth through his writing and talks. John's main focus and direct efforts, however, were toward clearing the name of Captain Piero Calamai, Master of the *Andrea Doria,* when it was hit by the *Stockholm,* and Captain Stanley Lord, who supposedly neglected to come to the aid of the passengers on the *Titanic* on her fateful voyage.

John and I worked together for twenty years to disseminate the truth and thereby exonerate Captain Calamai as the scapegoat of this disaster.

David Bright and I worked separately with John Carrothers on solving the supposed mystery of collision. We did not meet until John's death in 1991. Since then we worked closely on documentaries and scheduled *Andrea Doria* survivor reunions until his fatal dive to the *Andrea Doria* in 2006. I valued his friendship, advice and support. I will always miss him.

In addition, I owe much gratitude to the Discovery, National Geographic, A&E, History and PBS Channels for airing documentaries on the cause of the collision.

For technical support I wish to thank Marilyn Hetsel, Director of Simulation at the Computer Assisted Operational Research Facility (CAORF), U.S. Merchant Marine Academy in Kings Point NY. We spent hours on the bridge simulator on the approach of both vessels based on their course recorder graphs. The simulated approach validated what John Carrothers stated and believed was the rightful cause of this collision.

In appreciation for the working group composed of *Andrea Doria* officers, officials and professors. Their report in 1988 also validated John Carrothers theory on the cause of the collision. Captain Guido Badano of the working group was second officer of the *Andrea Doria* who I met during the 40th anniversary of the sinking with the survivors. His input and sharing of observations on the documentaries helped to further confirm the cause of this collision.

During *Andrea Doria* reunions, I have met many survivors including Pierette Simpson whose book <u>Alive on the *Andrea Doria*</u> gave further support to publicize the true cause of the collision.

Finally, no acknowledgement would be complete with mentioning my wife, Christine, who stood by me in this matter for the past 35 years. Her support and contributions were beyond the responsibilities of a wife and for which I will always be eternally grateful.

CHAPTER ONE

THE T/S ANDREA DORIA INBOUND TO NEW YORK

The *Andrea Doria* was the first truly opulent ocean liner that the Italian Line built following the decimation of its merchant fleet in World War II. Although it was not meant to be the largest transatlantic ocean liner, it was almost 700 feet long; not meant to be the fastest, it cruised at more than 24 knots. The *Andrea Doria* was built for beauty. Many people have called this ship the most beautiful ever built, and it was referred to by its builder, Ansaldo, as a floating art museum. For this renaissance of the Italian fleet, the Italian government commissioned its most famous artisans to design and build the various social rooms in a way that chronicled the distinguished history of Italy's contributions to the arts and sciences. The ship embodied the vibrant heart and soul of Italian heritage and its people; and it was loved by all who traveled on its decks.

What follows is an account of the approach to New York by the *Andrea Doria* on July 25, 1956. The information was gathered from John Carrothers, excerpts from Alvin Moscow's <u>Collision Course</u> and the round table discussions in Chapter Seven of this book.

About mid-afternoon on July 25, 1956, the senior officer of the watch on the Italian luxury liner *Andrea Doria*, inbound to New York from

Genoa, Italy, notified his commanding officer, Captain Piero Calamai, that fog was closing in rapidly around the ship. The captain went to the bridge and immediately ordered the ship's engines placed under standby conditions. The automatic timer had already been set to sound the fog whistle every two minutes.

On the bridge of the *Andrea Doria* the watch changed at 2000. The ship was surrounded by a thick opaque fog which cut visibility to one-half mile. Senior second officer Franchini, 37 years old, and junior third officer Giannini, age 28, assumed the watch with the ship's course as 267º. Captain Calamai and his two watch officers all possessed a master's license. Four seaman were also on watch; one being stationed on the forward end of the weather deck as a lookout.

The *Andrea Doria* was running with engines on standby at a speed reduced from 23 to 21.85 knots. Her engines were pounding out 35,000 horsepower. The turbines fed by high pressure steam turned the ship's two giant propellers, each 16 feet in diameter, at 135 RPM. The ship was 697 feet long, had a beam of 90 feet high and displaced over 29,000 tons. In reduced visibility the fog signal of one prolonged blast was automatically sounding every hundred seconds in accordance with the Rules of the Road.

The *Andrea Doria* was nearing the end of her 4,000 mile voyage from her home port of Genoa through the Straits of Gibraltar and then via the Great Circle route through the Azore Islands to Nantucket light ship which served as landfall for the United States and soon 1,134 passengers would disembark at New York.

The radar was in operation. A second radar was on standby, ready, in case the other radar had a casualty. As the *Andrea Doria* plowed through the misty wet fog, Captain Calamai, as was his practice, paced the bridge incessantly and though of the many times he had navigated his ship through fog during his forty-one round trip crossings of the north Atlantic.

Captain Calamai, age 58, was an excellent seaman and navigator. He was an introverted person who would rather be on the bridge than complying with the captain's social obligations. He was well respected, admired and liked by all his associates. Captain Calamai's father, Oresto, was the founder of the prestigious publication *The Italian Navy*. His brother, Paolo, was an admiral in the Italian Navy during World Wars I and II. During WWII, Lieutenant Commander Piero Calamai had won the Italian War Cross for saving his torpedoed battleship by running it aground.

Captain Calamai had made sure the water tight doors were closed when fog was first encountered at 1500 that afternoon and had been on the bridge since that time. He would remain there, eating his meals there, until visibility improved. Meanwhile, he would pace the twenty feet from the bridge door to the starboard wing glancing at the radar from time to time.

At 2120, third officer Giannini called out an observation of a pip on the radar scope 17 miles dead ahead. After careful observation and checking with the RDF[1], the contact was ascertained to be Nantucket light ship, the first checkpoint for the *Doria* since the Azore Islands. At 14 miles from the light ship, Captain Calamai ordered a course change from 267° to 261°.

On the bridge wing Captain Calamai peered out into the fog which enveloped the bulbous bow of his ship. If he were to obey the Rules which called for ships to be able to stop with half the distance of visibility, the Italian superliner should have been stopped dead in the water. But the *Andrea Doria* also had an obligation to dock her 1,134 passengers in New York early the next morning. About 250 longshoremen had been hired to be on the dock ready for work at 0800 and they would be paid from 0800 on, whether or not the ship arrived on time. Besides wasn't

---

1 Radio Frequency Finder tunes in radio frequencies of stations to obtain their bearing and the plot on a chart where they cross is called an "RDF" fix.

this a calculated risk that every master, especially of a passenger vessel, must take?

The fog grew thicker as the *Andrea Doria* approached the Nantucket light ship, an area where the warm Gulf Stream traveling up the east coast of the U.S. from Florida collides with the cold-water streams which originate in the Bay of Fundy off Nova Scotia.

At 2220, second officer Franchini calls out *"We are abeam of Nantucket – distance one mile."* The captain immediately ordered a course change to 268° which would take the ship 200 miles on a direct line to Ambrose light ship. In the chart room third officer Giannini recorded the fix and calculated the ship's speed as 21.8 knots.

At 2240, second officer Franchini observed a small pip 4° to starboard, bearing 272°, and distance 17 miles. It appeared, after a few minutes, that the contact was coming on an opposite and parallel course slightly to starboard of the *Doria*. Franchini concluded that since the radar bearing was increasing slowly to the right, that there would be a safe passing. Captain Calamai concurred.

Despite the Rules of the Road which required ships meeting head-on or nearly head-on to alter course to the right for a port to port passing, Captain Calamai believed there was sufficient passing distance for a starboard-to-starboard passing. As neither ship was in visual sight of the other, most mariners would concur with his decision under those circumstances. By staying to his left, Captain Calamai was keeping his ship toward the open sea rather than steering towards the dangers of shallower water and encounters with more contacts which might cause him to turn farther to the right and even closer to the shore. Without a plot, Captain Calamai did not realize that the combined speed of the two ships was 40 knots (two miles every three minutes).

2301: with the ships seven miles apart, second officer Franchini switched to the ten mile scale and now estimated the closest point of approach (CPA) to be about a mile to starboard in about ten minutes.

2303: Captain Calamai ordered a course change to 264° and "nothing to the right". Now the captain, followed by Giannini walked out to the starboard wing to listen for the foghorn of the other ship. All they heard was the prolonged blast of the *Doria's* fog signal every hundred seconds.

2308: Giannini strode into the wheelhouse for a glance at the radar. He saw the pip of the ship less than two miles off and about 30° to starboard. Snatching a pair of binoculars, Giannini went out to the starboard wing and along with the captain finally caught a glimpse of the glow of lights from the contact. (Figure 1)

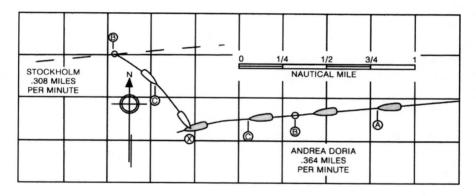

Figure 1. The *Andrea Doria's* contention.

A: Three minutes before collision, Captain Calamai joins Third Officer on the starboard bridge wing in order to visually see the approaching vessel.

B to B: 100 seconds before collision, glow of *Stockholm's* lights sighted. Believing ships on reciprocal course, *Andrea Doria* maintains course and speed.

C to C: About one minute before collision when ships exposed themselves to each other and their navigational lights became distinguishable, conditions were instantly recognized as being in extremis. Therefore, both ships resorted to Rule #27 as a last ditch effort to avoid immediate danger.

X: Collision seconds later.

Giannini was first to see the masthead lights. The forward light was to the right of the aft range light. But in the next instant the lights were coming in line. *"She is turning, she is turning!"* the young officer screamed. *"She is showing her red side light."* Captain Calamai couldn't believe it. The ship, now less than a mile away, was heading toward the *Doria*.

Captain Calamai called out *"Tutto sinistra"* (all left), and dashed to the center window. Franchini rushed to the fog signal and with the captain's permission switched off the automatic fog signal and sounded two sharp blasts for a left turn. He then ran to the EOT (engine order telegraph) but the captain yelled, *"No, do not touch the engines—she turns faster."* The ship began to turn as the gyrocompass could be heard to click off the degrees—two clicks for each degree. The giant liner began to swing crabwise on the water, the bow turning left first as the ship plunged forward. But it was too late.

The slender bow of this mysterious ship aimed directly at Captain Calamai as he stood now transfixed on the starboard bridge wing of his ship. At the last moment, instinct for self-preservation prevailed. Captain Calamai retreated toward the wheelhouse door. Then the *Stockholm* struck.

At practically full speed, the *Stockholm* plunged headlong halfway through the *Andrea Doria*, just as she was beginning to respond to her helm in the evasive hard-left turn that had just been ordered. The *Stockholm* entered the *Andrea Doria* at a point directly under the starboard bridge wing while Captain Calamai and his third officer looked on in horror. The *Andrea Doria* had been mortally wounded.

The force of the collision by the ice-reinforced bow of the *Stockholm* had breached the *Andrea Doria's* keel and her sinking was inevitable. Some eleven hours later the *Andrea Doria* sank in 240 feet of water.

Of the 1,706 souls aboard the *Andrea Doria* consisting of 1,134 passengers and 572 crew, 43 passengers were killed upon impact.

A four-year-old accidentally died during rescue as she was lowered into a lifeboat. One 14-year old girl, Linda Morgan, was transferred from her bunk to the jagged bow of the *Stockholm*. The bow's penetration killed her mother and step father but had scooped Linda up. After the *Stockholm* retreated from the side of the *Andrea Doria*, crewmen on the *Stockholm* found her with only a few scratches and bruises but still alive. She became the "miracle girl of the disaster."

The collision and sinking of the *Andrea Doria* marked the twilight of the ocean liner as a significant means for passage across the ocean. Within a year of this tragedy, the first transoceanic flights were routinely scheduled and replaced these greyhounds of the Atlantic as the major route of immigration to the New World. The demise of the *Andrea Doria* was also a major milestone in the advent of real-time media coverage of a historic event. The sinking was covered by all the world's leading media firms, and it was the first ocean liner sinking ever captured on film for the new medium called television. The *Stockholm's* destruction of Italy's maritime crown jewel had ramifications throughout the world and was a devastating loss to the country and its people.

CHAPTER TWO

THE M/V STOCKHOLM OUTBOUND FROM NEW YORK

The gleaming white motorship *Stockholm* of the Swedish American Lines was a 12,165 ton vessel with a length of 525 feet and a beam of 69 feet. Many of my Swedish relatives traveled to Sweden during the early 1950s and I had the opportunity to be aboard the *Stockholm* for departures. On one occasion I was able to meet Captain Nordenson. I was intimidated by his presence but also proud to be aboard such a magnificent Swedish ship.

She was built for comfort with seven decks and accommodations for 548 passengers. All the living spaces for passenger and crew provided for an outboard cabin. This beautiful yacht-like vessel was launched in 1948 and the fourth vessel named *Stockholm*. In the engine room two huge eight-cylinder diesel oil engines (total 14,600 hp) drove the ship's twin propellers at 110 RPM (revolutions per minute) and 18.5 knots when the engine order telegraph (EOT) pointed to full speed ahead. Her draft (keel to waterline) was 24 feet, 9 inches. That fateful July 25, 1956 was the 103rd eastbound crossing of the north Atlantic for this liner and the fourth crossing for 26 year old Ernst Carstens-Johannsen who was to be watch officer that evening from 2000-2400 (8:00 PM-midnight). The Master, Gunnar Nordenson, at 63 years of age, had 46 years of sea-life behind him and was a hard taskmaster. The

Stockholm, the smallest ship of the White Viking fleet of the Swedish Line was a compact tightly run vessel.

This account of the *Andrea Doria-Stockholm* collision disaster starts some twelve hours before the fatal tragedy when, at 11:30 on the morning of July 25, 1956, Captain Gunnar Nordenson, commanding officer of the *M/V Stockholm,* moved his ship away from her Swedish-American berth in New York and headed for the open sea and Europe.

At the same time, from a pier half mile downstream, Baron Raoul De Beaudean was executing the identical maneuver with his luxury liner *Ile de France*. Little did Captain De Beaudean realize the vital part his ship would play in the tragedy that would play out some twelve hours later on the Atlantic Ocean.

The *Stockholm* fell in behind the *Ile de France* as the ships worked their way to Ambrose Light at the main entrance to New York Harbor. Here they dropped their pilots shortly after 1:00 PM and set course toward Nantucket Lightship some 200 miles to the east.

The *Ile de France* at a speed of 22.5 knots was four knots faster than the *Stockholm.* By 3:00 PM she has pulled far ahead of the *Stockholm* and was rapidly disappearing from view.

The *Stockholm's* contention of how the accident happened was the antithesis of the *Andrea Doria's* account. Third officer, Carstens-Johannsen, who was in charge of the *Stockholm's* bridge at the time of the collision, gave the following account of what happened while under oath at the official inquiry. Following are excerpts of his testimony from the book Collision Course.

> When Carstens-Johannsen came to the bridge for his watch that evening the course was 090° due east from New York harbor's Ambrose light vessel to Nantucket light ship anchored off the shoals of Nantucket Island. His vessel was in an area known as "Times Square" due to the many arrivals and departures at

New York, one of the busiest ports in the world. Carstens-Johannsen had checked the chart and several messages, one of which indicated fog off Nantucket but it was not unusual for this time of the year. He was not that concerned as the captain was in his cabin below the pilot house. The radar was on with no visual ships and no radar contacts within the 15 mile range. The three seaman of Carstens-Johanssen's watch were taking turns in 80-minute periods as helmsman, lookout and standby. The average age of the four men was 22 years old. The helmsman Larsen, with six months experience in Swedish American Lines was deemed unreliable by Carstens-Johanssen himself.

Carstens-Johanssen was the only officer on the bridge. There was no smoking or coffee drinking permitted on the bridge of the *Stockholm*. Officers were not to fraternize with the seaman lest familiarity break down the chain of command rigidly adhered to on this ship. Conversation was limited to matters in the line of duty.

At 2100 Captain Nordenson came up for his postprandial look around. He responded to Carstens-Johanssen's greeting and continued his pacing. Carstens-Johanssen went about his duties without undue concern. He was not the worrying type. At 2130, having checked the chart the Captain told Carstens-Johanssen to change course to 087° to offset a southerly set. Carstens-Johanssen immediately relayed the order to the helmsman. At 2140 Carstens-Johanssen plotted his dead reckoning position and laying off his 087° track having calculated the *Stockholm* would pass Nantucket light ship three miles abeam to port.

The ship was riding easily, rolling slowly from side to side through undulating water. Occasionally the moon ducked behind a cloud but soon reappeared some two points (22½°) on the starboard bow. The night remained almost as warm as the day, about 70°, and both doors of the wheelhouse leading to the wings of the bridge were left open. Ordinarily the windward door was kept closed but this night there was only the slightest breeze from the southwest. Fog was usually prevalent with a southwest breeze. To pass the time Carstens-Johanssen switched the radar range from 15 to 50 miles which brought the coast of the U.S. on to the screen. He enjoyed trying to identify the various points of land.

At 2200 Captain Nordenson came into the wheelhouse from the bridge wing and announced he was going below to his cabin and would be there if needed. *"Call me when you see Nantucket,"* he told the third officer. Carstens-Johanssen quickly calculated that this would occur when he was being relieved since Nantucket light ship was about 40 miles ahead.

At 2204 Carstens-Johanssen obtained an RDF fix using Nantucket light ship and Block Island which checked out with a simultaneous fathometer reading of 35 fathoms. The ship was on track and a check of the radar revealed no contacts. For fixing the ship's position, the *Stockholm* did not have a long range and navigational system (LORAN). The *Andrea Doria* did have a LORAN to fix her position.

At 2230 Carstens-Johanssen took another RDF fix using Nantucket light ship, Block Island and Pollock Rip light ship. This time the position indicated the *Stockholm* was now 2.7 miles north of her track. To correct for this northerly set Carstens-Johanssen ordered a course change to 089°. Another RDF fix was taken at 2248 and now the *Stockholm's* position was plotted three miles north of the track. Carstens-Johanssen ordered another 2° course change to the right to a course of 091°. Carstens-Johanssen then checked the radar after his third RDF fix and noticed a pip (contact) just to the left of the heading flasher 12.0 miles away.

He decided to wait until the contact was 10 miles away. He would then begin plotting her on the luminescent maneuvering board set up beside the scope. Carstens-Johanssen adjusted the compass rose on the radar to 091° and when the contact was ten miles away marked his maneuvering board placing an X at a bearing of 089° range ten miles. (He noted the time in the logbook, later missing, but in the investigation later he could not recall the time.) The *Stockholm's* radar was not fitted with a gyrocompass as it was on the *Andrea Doria*. Carstens-Johanssen walked out to the wing of the bridge. The night, it seemed to Carstens-Johanssen, had not changed. The moon shone overhead and the sea remained calm.

At about 2300 as the bridge clock rang six bells, he obtained a radio direction bearing fix (RDF) entering the time as such in the ship's log book. As a result of this RDF fix, he found the *Stockholm* has drifted to the left, or north of her projected course. Therefore, he ordered a slight change in course to the right to correct, or compensate for this drift to left. The *Stockholm's* course recorder graph indicates a three-degree change in course to the right, from a compass heading of 92° to 95°, was executed at 2305. The third officer said that just as he ordered this compensating change in course following his 2300 RDF fix, he picked up the *Andrea Doria* at a distance of twelve miles by radar. He also said the radar target was bearing slightly over the *Stockholm's* port, or left bow.

Carstens-Johanssen stated the night was clear with good visibility and the engines were running under "all clear full speed ahead" orders.

This same third officer further stated that after the radar showed the distance between the ships had been reduced from twelve to ten miles he began a series of radar plots at regular intervals. Every radar plot confirmed the fact that it would be a port-to-port (left-side-to-left) meeting situation. Then, three minutes before the collision, the *Andrea*

Doria eventually exposed herself from out of a fogbank right at the point where his radar plotting told him she would appear. He then said that the *Andrea Doria* was showing a weak red port, or left-side light with masthead and range lights open. At this instant the radar told him the *Andrea Doria* was at a distance of 1.8 or 1.9 miles bearing between 15° and 25° over the *Stockholm's* port bow. Although there was ample room for a left-side-to-left-side meeting, he ordered a 22½ ° (2 point) right turn away from the *Andrea Doria* as a further precautionary measure.

While the *Stockholm* was executing this 22½ ° right turn, which the course recorder graph shows consumed two minutes, the telephone rang. After the *Stockholm* had steadied on her new heading, which the course recorder graph shows occurred one minute before the collision, the third officer Carsten-Johanssen again checked the *Andrea Doria's* lights and satisfied himself that she would now pass well astern of the *Stockholm*. He then turned away to answer the telephone.

Seconds later, at the end of the telephone conversation with the lookout in the crow's nest who reported "lights to port", he again checked the lights of the *Andrea Doria*. To his horror, he found the ships had totally changed relative positions. The *Andrea Doria* was not showing her green, or right starboard, side light as she was attempting to race across the *Stockholm's* bow. Realizing instantly that conditions were in extremis, he ordered a hard-right turn and rang up an all-out emergency, full-speed astern on the engine order telegraphs. It was apparent that the *Stockholm* had slowed down little, if any, before plunging headlong into the *Andrea Doria's* starboard side. The *Stockholm* was not on standby engines and the motorman on watch was not immediately available to respond to the full speed astern order.

Ernst Carstens-Johannsen, as third officer, contended that he did not see the *Andrea Doria* cut across the *Stockholm's* bow because he had taken his eyes off her to answer the telephone. However, the lookout in the crow's nest alleged under oath that after his telephone conversation with this third officer he watched the *Andrea Doria* close out her red port side light and show her green starboard side light as she turned to her left in an attempt to race across the *Stockholm's* bow. For this to occur it would have necessitated the *Andrea Doria* to execute an "S" turn and increase her speed to 2,500 mph. (See Figure 2)

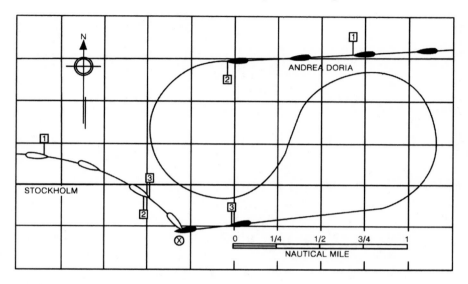

Figure 2. The *Andrea Doria's* 2,500 mph "S" turn.

[1] to [1] Three minutes before collision. The *Doria* appears out of fog at a distance of 1.85 miles on *Stockholm's* port bow. Turn to starboard of 22.5° ordered by Carstens Johannsen. [2] to [2] One minute before collision *Stockholm* completes right turn. Carstens Johannsen checks *Doria's* lights, turns to answer telephone. [3] to [3] Seconds later Carstens Johannsen finds *Doria* in collision course, attempting to race across his bow. Hard right and full speed astern ordered. [X] Collision.

Shows that the *Andrea Doria*, in order to get from her point [2], where the *Stockholm's* third officer placed her one minute before the collision, to point [3], where he put her seconds later, would have had to execute an enormous "S" turn and attain a speed in excess of 2,500 mph.

To refute the 2,500 mph "S" turn and to corroborate Carstens-Johanssen visual sighting of the *Andrea Doria's* red port side light over the *Stockholm's* port bow, the *Stockholm* owners contended that the approach of both vessels was as depicted in Figure 3.

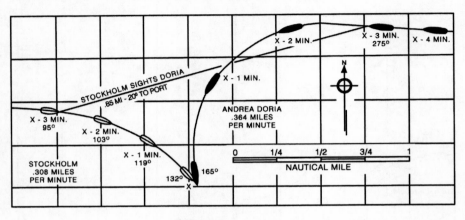

Figure 3. The Long 3-Minute Turn. *Stockholm's* owners contend, as depicted, that both ships started their turns three minutes before the collision, which occurred at the end of the turns when the ships were on the headings indicated. Still, as can be seen by noting the distance between the *Doria's* positions in the period from X-4 to X-3 minutes and comparing them with the distances between for the three minutes following, she would have had to instantaneously double her speed in order to reach the collision point.

Both ships started their turns three minutes before the collision, which occurred at the end of the turns when the ships were on the headings indicated. The *Andrea Doria* executed a long three-minute turn of 110 degrees to port going from a compass heading of 275° degrees to a heading of 165°. The accident happened at the end of this long port turn.

Figure 3 is an illustration of this contention. The *Andrea Doria's* reduced speed of 21.85 knots is indicated in the one-minute (X-4 Min) period prior to X-3 Min. She would have been required to double her speed to reach this collision position. Furthermore, in no way can the condition of the *Stockholm's* bow after the collision be reconciled to the roll-type collision illustrated here.

Finally, the Swedish American Line claims that the *Stockholm* by plunging into the starboard side of the *Andrea Doria* "*broke the left turn and pivoted the ship to the right.*" However, Figure 4 clearly shows that the *Stockholm* plunged into the *Andrea Doria* at a point far forward of the pivotal point. Therefore, she would have been thrust further on her left turn and certainly not pivoted to the right.

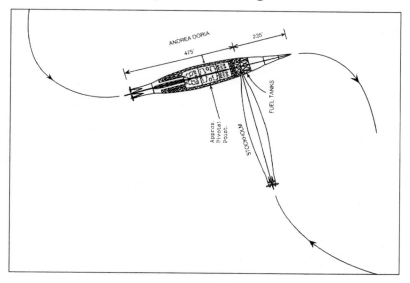

Figure 4. Collision point in relation to the pivotal point of the *Andrea Doria*.

Figures 1, 2, 3 and 4 are Courtesy of John Carrothers

CRUX OF THE *STOCKHOLM'S* DEFENSE

A monumental factor in the *Stockholm's* overall defense hinged on the answer to the vital question of what time did the third officer alter the ship's course to compensate for drift he found as the result of his 2300 RDF fix? Under oath, third officer Carstens-Johanssen testified that he picked up the *Andrea Doria* by radar at a distance of twelve miles, just as he ordered a slight change in course following his 2300 RDF fix. The *Stockholm's* course recorder graph shows a three-degree change in course from 92° to 95° was ordered at 2305 plus or minus seconds.

In cross examination the attorneys were quick to point out to the third officer that his testimony was "impossible and untrue." In effect they proved to him that at 2305, when he ordered the slight change in course to compensate for drift he found as the result of his 2300 RDF fix, the *Andrea Doria* was only four, and not twelve, miles away from the *Stockholm.*

Faced with this irrefutable fact the third officer simply explained that the 2300 entry he made in the *Stockholm's* log book at the time of the accident should have been "about 2300." Furthermore, he continued that he did not change course at 2305. This indication on his course recorder graph was only a "yaw"[2] in the ship's steering. He also claimed that the Sperry expert, who had identified the change in course at 2305, was wrong. The attorneys apparently accepted this explanation because, as far as could be determined, the issue was not mentioned again.

The third officer's denial of the 2305 change in course placed him in an untenable position. Now it was necessary to revert to the last previous slight change in course at 2240 (obviously made as the result of drift found in his 2230 RDF fix) as the time he picked up the *Andrea Doria* by radar at a distance of twelve miles. After informing his readers of this in his book, <u>Collision Course,</u> Mr. Moscow continued that by calculations the "about 2300" RDF fix was actually taken at 2248. It was as a result of drift found at 2248, writes Mr. Moscow, that the third officer altered course at 2240. Neither of these contentions is acceptable. At 2240 the ships were 20.66 miles and not twelve miles apart. How could the third officer alter course at 2240 to compensate for drift he did not know existed

---

2 Yaw is a deviation in the ship's heading due to the effects of wind and/or seas. A yaw should be noticeable to a helmsman and usually quite easy to correct by a little left or right rudder.

until eight minutes later at 2248? These alleged facts were presented by the third officer's testimony, which allegedly "correlated closely" with the *Stockholm's* course recorder graph. They cover the last hour before the collision and are presented in chronological order so that the sequence of events may be better understood.

- At 2220 the third officer altered course from a compass heading of 87° to 89° to compensate for drift found twenty minutes later as the result of his 2230 RDF fix.

- The third officer picked up the *Andrea Doria* by radar at a distance twelve miles just as he ordered a slight change in course from a compass heading of 89° to 91° at 2240 to correct for drift found eight minutes later as the result of his 2248 RDF fix which he thought was "about 2300" (At 2240 the ships were 20.66 miles apart.)

- The third officer waited for three minutes, until the distance between the ships had been reduced to ten miles, before starting to plot the oncoming *Andrea Doria* by radar. Note: to correlate the *Andrea Doria's* actions with the foregoing, while recognizing that the *Stockholm* was running at a speed of 18.5 knots, it would have been necessary for the *Andrea Doria* to have increased her speed to 194.72 knots to reduce the distance between the ships from 20.66 to 10 miles in three minutes. The *Andrea Doria* would then have resumed her normal speed of 21.85 knots when the third officer allegedly started his plotting procedures.

- The third officer then plotted the oncoming *Andrea Doria* at the regular and prescribed intervals until, three minutes before the collision, the *Andrea Doria* finally exposed herself from out of the fog right at the spot where his radar plotting told him she would appear.

These contradictions are displayed in Table 1 where it is apparent that the *Stockholm's* version does not correlate with the course recorder graph. As the course recorder graphs were not presented in evidence for litigation this was never clarified. Facts are facts however, and they not cease to exist because they are ignored.

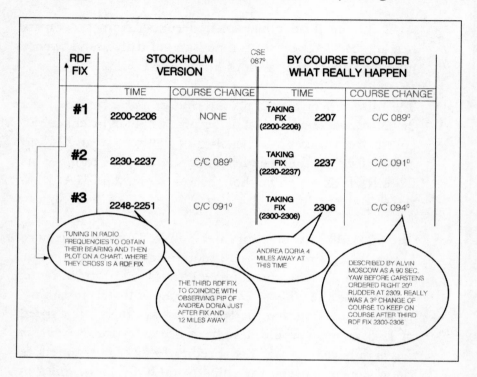

Table 1. Correlation of testimony and course recorder graph.

CHAPTER THREE

COLLISION AND THE FATAL ERROR

2322: <u>Eleven Minutes After Impact.</u> The *Stockholm* was dislodged from the side of the *Andrea Doria* from the twisting action generated by the *Doria's* forward momentum. The fact that there was no fire despite the sparks as the *Stockholm* was wrenched free of her penetration was amazing. The penetration was estimated to be 30 feet within the upper deck, 18 feet at the water level (C deck) and seven feet into the double bottoms.

Captain Calamai, feeling several bumps, ran out to the starboard bridge wing to see the *Stockholm* disappear astern. The *Andrea Doria* immediately took a list 18° to starboard. The list renders her port side lifeboats useless and the launching of her starboard lifeboats a dangerous and hazardous operation.

In an excerpt from <u>Collision Course</u>, the impact area was described as follows: *"In smashing open the deep tank compartment, the Stockholm had struck a vulnerable spot. Her bow pierced the five fuel tanks on the starboard side of the compartment and left intact the portside tanks. The ten fuel tanks near the end of the voyage had been empty and not refilled with ballast since refueling had been scheduled for the next morning and deballasting would have taken too long.*

(a) Thus, some 500 tons or 240,000 gallons of sea water gushed into the starboard tanks, providing that much dead weight on one side of the ship, while the air-filled port tanks rose out of the sea like a balloon.

(b) The greater the list to starboard, the more hundreds and thousands of tons of water poured into the 40 foot hole in the side of the Doria. As water rushed in, the ship's list kept increasing.

(c) It seemed only a matter of time before the ship would roll over on her starboard side and go down. The Andrea Doria was doomed."

Nearby the *Stockholm* was shrouded in fog and each vessel could faintly see the glow of each other's lights. They remained unidentified to each other. The sea is oily calm.

The *Stockholm* had 748 persons on board. With 75 feet of her bow demolished she is in a precarious position. In addition, she is unable to move because her anchors had dropped in the collision and the machinery used to hoist them had been destroyed. It was to be several hours before the chains could be cut to release her.

At collision plus eleven minutes, *Stockholm's* radio opens up with: "CQ—CQ—C Q" (attention all stations), "XXX—XXX—XXX" (stand by for urgent message), "DE—SEJT" (*Stockholm's* radio call letters). With *Stockholm* still transmitting *Andrea Doria* breaks in actuating automatic alarm signals on 500 kilocycles (picked up by ships and shore stations all over the world) before transmitting: "CQD—CQD—C QD" (attention all stations), "SOS—SOS—SOS—DE—ICEH."

The United States Coast Guard Search and Rescue New York assumes command. Their radio network between Boston and New Orleans; Clears teletype lines between stations and bases: Eastern Sea Frontier Coast Guard Base placed on "Standby – at the ready alert." Seven minutes later *Andrea Doria* transmits distress position. In Appendix 1 are the more pertinent transmissions were lifted from the hundreds of intercommunication messages recorded during the sinking.

Throughout the drama the voice of the U.S. Coast Guard was heard constantly directing and coordinating the rescue efforts. Eight cutters were at the scene with three more racing to location when the area was cleared. The cutters on scene patrolled the waters searching for survivors and assisting in every possible way in their efforts to save human life.

No account of this tragedy would be complete without a justly deserved "well done" to this agency who took command and coordinated this rescue effort.

The Sperry Course Recorder Graphs

Carstens-Johannsen, the *Stockholm's* third officer, claimed the night was clear. Captain Calamai, of the *Andrea Doria*, said the fog was thick with visibility reduced to less than one mile. The *Stockholm's* third officer contended that the entire radar approach and initial visual sighting was a left side to left side passing and had the *Andrea Doria* not suddenly executed a hard left turn, after she had been sighted three minutes before the collision, the accident never would have happened. Captain Calamai declared that the entire radar approach and initial visual sighting was a right side to right side passing and, had the *Stockholm* not executed a hard right turn during the final three minutes, there never would have been a collision. Obviously we are confronted with an impossible situation.

There appeared to be something very wrong with the *Stockholm's* contention for several reasons. The *Andrea Doria's* version was the only one to make any sense. In order to clear up this controversy or impossible situation we refer to the Sperry Gyrocompass Course Recorder Graphs, the most important pieces of documentary evidence presented by each ship at the official inquiry. The absolute integrity of this recording instrument has never been questioned let alone challenged.

With these course recorder graphs, along with the known speed of the ships, it was a simple matter to produce a plot, or diagram, illustrating precisely how not why but how the ships entered the collision. Had there been a Coast Guard, or Naval Board of Inquiry following this incident undoubtedly the first order of business would have been to produce such a plot. Then as each witness' testimony would be compared, or correlated with the facts scribed on their own course recorder graph. It is not an exaggeration to say that with such a Coast Guard, or Naval Board of inquiry the question of right-to-right or left-to-left would have been solved in no more than a couple of hours.

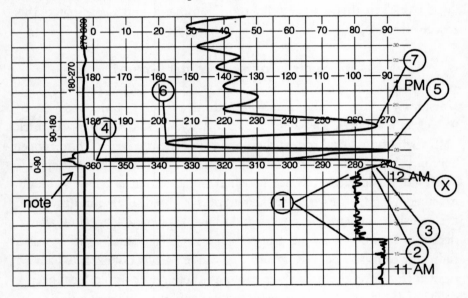

Figure 5a

Andrea Doria

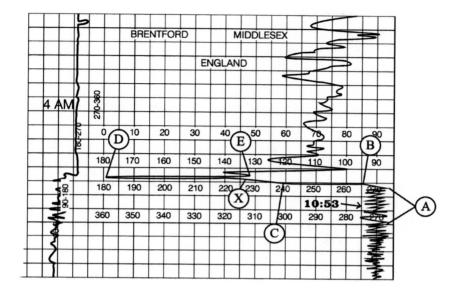

Figure 5b

Stockholm

The thick vertical line scribed in the left margin of the course recorder graphs of the *Andrea Doria* and the *Stockholm* indicates which of the four 90° quadrants is to be used in reading the ship's heading that is being recorded by the other thick vertical line at the right side of the graph. The *Doria's* graph, for example, shows the collision approach to have been recorded in the 270°-360° quadrant column. By reading the quadrant, it can be seen that the *Doria* had been on a heading of 279° for about 43 minutes preceding the collision.

A 10° error in synchronization between the *Andrea Doria's* gyrocompass and course recorder was detected, proved, admitted, and explained by her captain. This error is reflected throughout the plot; i.e., the plot shows the *Andrea Doria* on a heading of 269° at 11:05. Her graphs show a heading of 279° at the same time. Also, the *Stockholm's* graph shows the collision at 03.11, the *Andrea Doria's* at 12.11 while the actual zone time was 23.11. This discrepancy is of no consequence, because in producing a plot, the ships are placed in their respective collision positions at the moment of impact. Then, with each horizontal line representing a period of ten minutes, the plot can be worked back minute by minute to a point as far as is necessary to determine just how the ships entered the collision.

The *Stockholm's* course recorder graph clearly shows the lack of concentration of the ship's helmsman in approaching the collision point. The two starboard turns appears opposite on a course recorder graph. By working backward from the collision point, it is clear that the *Stockholm's* third officer was mistaken about when he said he first visually detected the *Andrea Doria*.

The tremendous impact caused the course recorder pen to jump up and down clearly showing the collision point [X] on each graph.

[X] at collision the *Andrea Doria* (in a left turn) was heading 262º and the *Stockholm* (in a hard right turn) was heading 132º.

Stockholm Graph

(A)   On course 091º since correction for 2240 RDF fix. Note yawing by helmsman.

(B)   2305 Carstens-Johannsen orders right turn of 22½ º to about 115º

(C)   About 2308 Carstens-Johannsen sees the *Andrea Doria* green side light and orders hard right

(X)   Collision.

(D, E) Drifting after collision

Note: Course changes look opposite on a course recorder graph so that Carstens-Johannsen turn to starboard appears to be a left turn.

Andrea Doria Graph

(1)   Course correction 269°T which shows as 279° due to 10° error synchronization error between gyrocompass recording and course recorder graph. Also, time is one hour behind so course change is at 2220 showing as 1120 a.m. on graph, not 2320. Despite this, the above still represents the approach of the *Andrea Doria*.

(2)   2303 *Doria* changes course to 264° to open up passing distance (shows as 0003 on graph).

(3)   2309 *Doria* orders hard left

(X)   Collision

(4, 5, 6, 7) Indicates drifting not under control after collision

Illustrated in Figure 5 are the course recorder graphs and interpretation of how the collision happened according to these graphs. For quick reference the plot in Figure 6 has been captioned with the pertinent testimony of the two key witnesses. A plot comparable to this was endorsed by Captain Philip Van Horn Weems, U.S.N. (Ret) at the Naval Institute in Annapolis. Over his signature Captain Weems wrote that, in his opinion, the plot correlated with the course recorder graphs to within about one degree and plus or minus seconds.

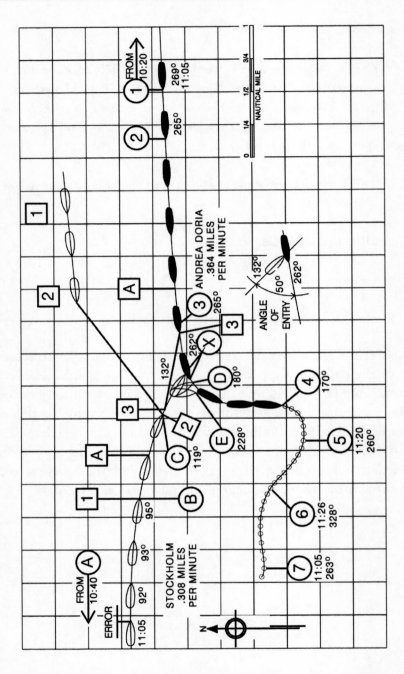

Figure 6. Approach of *Andrea Doria* and *Stockholm* which correlates with the course recorder graphs. Courtesy of John Carrothers.

In the author's plotted interpretation (above) of the Sperry Gyrocompass Course Recorder graphs, the circled symbols match those on the course recorder graphs and the squared symbols represents the conflicting testimony.

Andrea Doria's Testimony		*Stockholm's* Testimony	
A to A	Capt. Calamai and his third officer sight glow of the *Stockholm's* lights. Believing the ships to be on parallel courses, the *Doria's* captain maintains speed & course.	*1 to 1*	Third officer sights the *Andrea Doria* at a distance of 1.8 miles, being 20° over the his ship's port bow, and orders 22½° right turn.
		2 to 2	The *Stockholm* completes right turn and third officer checks the *Doria's* lights. He then turns to answer the telephone.
3 to 3	Seeing that the *Stockholm* is turning sharply to her right—towards and into their ship—Capt Calamai orders hard left and maintains speed on engines.	*3 to 3*	Seconds later, third officer finishes telephone conversation and again checks the *Doria's* lights. He now finds the *Doria* in a collision situation and is attempting to race the *Stockholm's* bow. He orders hard right turn and full speed astern on both engines.
(X)	The collision with the *Stockholm* occurs just as the *Andrea Doria* begins to answer her helm.		
		(X)	The collision occurs with the *Andrea Doria* after the *Stockholm* has turned 13 degrees.

Captain Calamai's testimony correlates with what has been scribed on his course recorder graph as illustrated in Figure 1. This also coincides with his contention of how the accident happened as illustrated in *The New York Times*. By the same token it does not validate Carstens-Johannsen's testimony up to one minute before the collision. Then, for the final minute both ships agree to the letter with respect to what is displayed on their course recorder graphs.

It's impossible to accept the *Stockholm's* third officer's testimony that the colossal "S" turn as demonstrated in Figure 2, executed at a speed in excess of 2500 miles per hour by the *Andrea Doria*, was accomplished during the few seconds this third officer had taken his eyes off her to answer the telephone.

The *Stockholm's* third officer's testimony then stated that the *Andrea Doria* did not start her long left turn until after the *Stockholm* had completed her 22½° right one minute before the collision. (Figure 3)

The Swedish Line and Charles Haight, its attorney, claimed that both ships started their respective right and left turns simultaneously three minutes before the collision. If this were true the *Andrea Doria* would have had to double her speed from two minutes before the collision and the subsequent damage would not have been as disastrous as the near perpendicular collision was.

In this long left turn by the *Andrea Doria* lies the controversy. The *Andrea Doria* claimed she was hit at the start of this turn (Figure 1, point X). The *Stockholm* claimed the collision happened at the end of this same long left turn (Figure 3, point X).

The following excerpt from The Naval Institute Proceedings by John Carrothers is illustrated in Figure 6.

"At the official inquiry the testimony of the two prime witnesses was in total conflict even to the point as to where each claimed to have first observed the other appearing out of the fog. Ernst Carstens-Johannsen, the *Stockholm's* Third Officer, who was in charge of her bridge at the time of the collision, testified that he saw the *Andrea Doria* appear from out of the fog over the *Stockholm's* port bow. At the same time, Captain Piero Calamai, of the *Andrea Doria*, claimed that when the *Stockholm* appeared from out of the fog he saw her over the *Andrea Doria's* starboard bow. These were visual sightings; thus, any possibility of malfunction of the radar equipment must be ruled out.

Contradictions

Common sense dictates that when two ships are approaching each other on reciprocal courses, the passing must be either starboard-to-starboard or port-to-port. The testimony of the two men in charge of their respective bridges at the time of the collision contradicts this reasoning. The only possible conclusion is that one witness is correct and one witness is incorrect. There is no room for compromise. Fortunately, there exist two vital documents upon which is inscribed the fully story of how the ships arrived at the collision. These documents are the Sperry Gyro-compass Course Recorder graphs (Figure 5) which had been officially presented by both defendants and recorded by the Court as evidence.

In reconstructing collision cases, strandings, or any maritime casualty where navigation is involved, all that the U.S. Coast Guard or Navy requires are the Course Recorder graphs and the testified speed of the ships involved. Through the interpretation of these known factors, the events leading up to a casualty can be accurately determined. The absolute integrity of this Sperry instrument has never been questioned, let alone challenged.

As previously mentioned, had this inquiry been conducted under the jurisdiction of the U.S. Coast Guard or Navy, the first order of business undoubtedly would have been to produce a plot or diagram illustrating that which was scribed on the graphs. As each witness testified, his testimony then would have been compared with the graph's evidence. In this manner the correct answers would have been apparent. But this was not done, since neither the U.S. Coast Guard nor the Navy investigated the collision which involved two foreign ships in international waters and was therefore not under their jurisdiction. Let us, then, reproduce a plot of our own.

The plot (Figure 6) is to scale and has been worked back minute by minute from 11:11 PM to 11:04 PM where the actual collision sequences began. All this would seem to indicate that the *Stockholm's* radar equipment was operating on the five-mile range, which the third officer considered it to be operating on the 15-mile range, as can be seen in Figure 7. A target four miles distant on the five-mile range setting would appear on the identical spot on the radar's screen as one on the same bearing would have if she were 12 miles away on the

15-mile setting. (Figure 7) The third officer also said that the target was slightly to the left of the *Stockholm's* heading flasher (course line indicator on screen). The radar target was actually slightly to the right of the heading flasher. The two broken lines illustrate how the *Stockholm* was yawing to the right and left of her projected course as indicated on her graph. With this constant yawing, it is plain to see how the target would jump from one side to the other of the ship's projected course line or heading flasher.

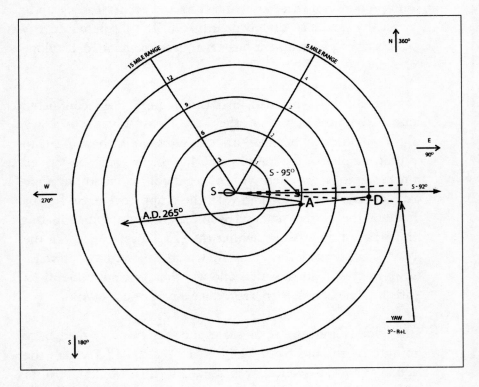

Figure 7. The Fatal Error

Facsimile of *Stockholm's* radar screen. Five mile range each circle carries a value of one mile. On the 15 mile range each circle is valued at three miles. Diagram produced from Figure 6. Broken lines illustrate how the graph showed the *Stockholm* was yawing 3° to port and starboard of her compass heading of 92°.

"S" to "D": Six minutes before collision. *Stockholm* allegedly picked up *Andrea Doria* at a distance of twelve miles bearing slightly over the *Stockholm's* port, or left, bow. Actually the *Andrea Doria* was only four miles away bearing slightly over the *Stockholm's* starboard, or right, bow. The only explanation for this is the error in radar range while the constant yawing caused the target to move back and forth from the port to starboard sides of the heading flasher of 92°. Note: with respect to distance it can be seen that the target appears in the identical spot on the screen in both the 5 and 15 mile ranges.

"S" to "A": Three minutes before the collision. *Stockholm* is now on a heading of 95°. Third officer assumes the *Andrea Doria* is six miles away while in reality she was only two miles distant. At this point, he ordered the 22½ ° right turn which ended in disaster less than three minutes later.

The Fatal Error

Carstens-Johannsen also testified that the target was coming towards the *Stockholm* at great speed. This, he said, led him to believe that the target might be some sort of naval vessel on manoeuvres. Then, three minutes before the collision, when the radar target had actually closed from a distance of four to two miles (while through his misinterpretation he thought the target had closed from 12 to six miles – thus indicating great speed) Carstens-Johannsen committed what appears to be the fatal error. It was at this moment that he ordered the 22½° change in course to the right which brought the *Stockholm* into the collision situation with the *Andrea Doria*.

Had the *Andrea Doria* actually been at a distance of six miles, instead of the two miles that she was, three minutes before the collision, the *Stockholm's* third officer's action in ordering this 22½° turn to starboard would have been absolutely correct according to the rules for using radar as an aid to navigation. Here the rule is: When a radar target appears dead (or nearly dead) ahead, make an early and substantial change in course, preferably to the right, in ample time for your action to show clearly on the other ship's radar screen. With the elimination of any other ship being present in the immediate area, this is the only other logical reason for Carstens-Johannsen to order such a bold change in course.

After the *Stockholm* had leveled off from the 22½° right turn, which was about one minute before the collision, the third officer said that he momentarily removed his eyes from the *Andrea Doria* to answer the telephone. At the conclusion of this telephone conversation, which had been from the lookout in the crow's nest reporting the lights, he found that the ships had totally changed relative positions. Now, he said, the *Andrea Doria* was in a collision situation attempting to race across the *Stockholm's* bow. From this point on, right up to the collision, the testimony, as given by both ships and the documentary evidence scribed on their graphs, dovetails in every respect. Thus, the testimony and graphs have established that the first time that Carstens-Johannsen could possibly have seen the *Andrea Doria* was about one minute before the collision after he had completed the 22½° right turn. It also establishes that the order of this 22½° right turn three minutes before the collision was the final cause of the disaster.

At the official inquiry, Carstens-Johannsen testified that he had changed the range on his radar equipment from the five-mile to the 15-mile to the 50-mile ranges from time to time during the course of his watch. When one considers that the range in radar equipment is changed with the turn of a dial, as one would change channels on a television set, it is understandable how easy it would be, in the pitch black of a darkened wheelhouse, to commit such an error. This is not an infrequent kind of error; however, in the majority of cases, it is detected before any damage is done. Nevertheless, it could account for the all-too-many collisions in which ships find themselves approaching each other in the fog on starboard-to-starboard reciprocal courses which terminate in right-angle type collisions.

Accidents are Caused

For those whose prime interest in accident cases is safety and education, there is no satisfaction in pointing the finger of guilt. Yet, facts are facts, and they have an eloquence of their own. Accidents don't just happen; they are caused. By examining the causes, valuable lessons can always be learned, by and for the men who are and will be in charge of the watch on the bridges of ships."

CHAPTER FOUR

COMPLIANCE WITH THE RULES OF THE ROAD

J ust as there are rules and regulations for driving automobiles so there are with vessel conduct on the high seas. These rules apply to all vessels and, in addition, many nations have such rules that are applicable to their inland waters. The international rules commonly called COLREGS (Collision Requirements) were applicable to the *Andrea Doria* and *Stockholm* who collided in international waters. The latest version of COLREGS became effective in 1977, but referred to as the 72 COLREGS. The Rules of the Road were basically the same as those that were in effect in 1956. The rule numbers are now different and wording such as burden for the give-way vessel and privilege for the stand-on vessel were utilized but the intent to prevent collision at sea is identical.

In 1948, the Safety of Life at Sea (SOLAS) International Conference included recognition of radar and its use to aid in the prevention of collisions had become effective in 1954 two years prior to the collision. The Rules of the Road now has 38 Rules and are listed in the following parts:

Part A   General

                Rule 1   Application

                Rule 2   Responsibility

                Rule 3   General Definitions

Part B   Steering and Sailing Rules

                            Section 1   In Any Visibility – Rules 4-10
                            Section 2   Vessels   in   Sight   of   One
                                         Another   –   Rules   11-18
                            Section 3   In   Restricted   Visibility
                                         – Rule 19

Part C   Lights and Shapes – Rules 20-31

Part D   Sound and Light Signals – Rules 32-37

Part E   Exemption – Rule 38

Annex I – IV

Of concern to this collision are: Vessels in Sight of One Another
(Rules 11-18)

                Rule 15   Crossing Situation

                Rule 16   Action by the Give-way Vessel

                Rule 17   Action by the Stand-on Vessel

These rules applied to both the *Andrea Doria* and *Stockholm* in the last
100 seconds when both vessels *had each other in visual sight*. Prior to

that point, Rule 19, Conduct of Vessels in Restricted Visibility was the applicable rule.

These rules stated the following:

Rule 15   Crossing Situation

When two power-driven vessels are crossing so as to involve risk of collision, the vessel which has the other on her own starboard side shall keep out of the way and shall, if the circumstances of the case admit, avoid crossing ahead of the other vessel.

Rule 16   Action by the Give-way Vessel

Every vessel that is directed to keep out of the way of another vessel shall, so far as possible, take early and substantial action to keep well clear.

Rule 17   Action by the Stand-on Vessel

(a)(i)   Where one of two vessels is to keep out of the way the other shall keep her course and speed.

(ii)   The latter vessel may however take action to avoid collision by her maneuver alone, as soon as it becomes apparent to her that the vessel required to keep out of the way is not taking appropriate action in compliance with these rules.

(b)   When, from any cause, the vessel required to keep her course and speed finds herself so close that collision cannot be avoided by the action of the give-way vessel alone, she shall take such action as will best aid to avoid collision.

(c)   A power-driven vessel which takes action in a crossing situation in accordance with subparagraph (a)(ii) of this rule to avoid collision with another power-driven vessel shall, if the circumstances of the case admit, not alter course to port for a vessel on her own port side.

(d)   This rule does not relieve the give-way vessel of her obligation to keep out of the way.

Note: When in visual sight of each other, the *Andrea Doria* became the give-way vessel and in accordance with Rule 17(a) ii, she may take action to avoid collision by her maneuver alone as soon as it becomes apparent to her that the stand-on vessel, *Stockholm*, was not take appropriate action in compliance with the Rules.

Rule 19   Conduct of Vessels in Restricted Visibility

(a)   This rule applies to vessels not in sight of one another when navigating in or near an area of restricted visibility.

(b)   Every vessel shall proceed at a safe speed adapted to the prevailing circumstances and conditions of restricted visibility. A power-driven vessel shall have her engines ready for immediate maneuver.

(c)   Every vessel shall have due regard to the prevailing circumstances and conditions of restricted visibility when complying with the rules of Section I of this part.

(d)   A vessel which detects by radar alone the presence of another vessel shall determine if a close-quarters situation is developing and/or risk of collision exists. If so, she shall take avoiding action in ample time, provided that when such action consists of an alteration of course, so far as possible the following shall be avoided:

(i)   an alteration of course to port for a vessel forward of the beam, other than for a vessel being overtaken;

(ii)   an alteration of course towards a vessel abeam of abaft the beam.

(e)   Except where it has been determined that a risk of collision does not exist, every vessel which hears apparently forward of her beam the fog signal of another vessel, or which cannot avoid a close-quarters situation with another vessel forward of her beam, shall reduce her speed to the minimum at which she can be kept on her course. She shall, if necessary, take all her way off and in any event navigate with extreme caution until danger of collision is over.

In his interview with *The New Haven Register*, the author of <u>Collision Course</u> declared: "The Rules of the Road state that when on a collision course, you should turn to the right. The *Andrea Doria* turned to the left."

As a result of this apparent violation of the Rules of the Road, the author asserted that he found Captain Calamai ". . . at fault". Thus, through a single statement Alvin Moscow indicted the captain of the *Andrea Doria* for not only being responsible for the collision but also for the loss of 51 human lives.

Let us now review the circumstances and conditions that existed during the final one hundred seconds when both vessels were in sight of each other and during which Captain Calamai allegedly violated the Rules of the Road when he ordered the hard left turn.

About one minute before the collision, when the ships' running lights became distinguishable to each other, the *Andrea Doria* found that the *Stockholm* was turning sharply to her right—toward and into the *Andrea Doria*. The *Stockholm* was showing the *Andrea Doria* her red left, or port, side light. The *Andrea Doria*, now approaching from the *Stockholm's* left, was in a collision situation that would place her directly in front of the oncoming *Stockholm*. The *Andrea Doria* was showing the *Stockholm* her green, or starboard, side light. Under normal circumstances and conditions, Rule #15 would designate the *Andrea Doria* as the "give-way" ship with the *Stockholm* being the "stand-on" ship.

Rule #15 required the *Andrea Doria*, as the give-way ship, to turn right and pass around the stern of the privileged ship. If this is not possible, the give-way ship must slow down and if necessary stop to allow the stand-on ship to pass in front of her. The stand-on ship, in accordance with Rule #17 simply maintains course and speed.

At the moment of initial visual sighting both ships instantly recognized that circumstances and conditions were in extremis. Therefore, both ships resorted to Rule #2 which states that: "In obeying these Rules due regard shall be had to all dangers of navigation and collision, and to any special circumstances, including the limitations of the craft involved, which may render a departure from the above Rules necessary in order to avoid immediate danger." Clearly this means that a ship may resort to any maneuver necessary in order "to avoid immediate danger."

Consider Captain Calamai's actions during this final minute. There were three vital facts about which he had full knowledge: (1) the *Andrea Doria* was advancing slightly more than three ship lengths per minute; (2) his ship would advance at least a full ship length after ordering any turn and then she would only respond slowly at first; (3) that it would require at least two miles to stop the *Andrea Doria* and more than a half mile to even begin to slow her down. With just three ship lengths left between him and disaster he saw at a glance that an early and substantial action, done in accordance with Rule #16, would turn him directly into a collision. Therefore, without hesitation he ordered the hard left turn and maintained the speed on his engines in the hope and prayer that some miracle would carry him safely across the *Stockholm's* bow. He also must have prayed that the *Stockholm* would have recognized the in extremis situation and would be acting accordingly in accordance with Rule #17 concerning the stand-on vessel.

After the *Stockholm* had leveled off from her 22½° right turn about one minute before the collision, Carstens-Johannsen found the *Andrea Doria* to be in a collision situation attempting to race across the *Stockholm's* bow. Recognizing at a glance that the situation was in extremis he ordered a hard right turn and an all out emergency *"full speed astern"* on both engines. Had the *Stockholm's* engines been operating under *"stand by"* orders instead of *"All Clear Full Speed Ahead"*, when these emergency orders were given, Captain Calamai's prayers would have been answered. All the *Andrea Doria* needed was another 15 seconds to safely get across the bow of the *Stockholm*.

While Captain Calamai prayed that he might get safely across the *Stockholm's* bow, the *Stockholm's* third officer saw that a collision was unavoidable. By ordering the hard right turn he hoped the *Stockholm* would be turning sufficiently to her right so that the ships would only roll on each other's sides rather than collide head on into the *Andrea Doria's* side. It is obvious that both ships acted correctly and abided to the letter concerning the Rules of the Road when conditions were found to be in extremis.

The Rule which took precedent over everything related to this disaster was Rule #19, governing speed in restricted visibility. This Rule, the nemesis of every person who has ever been in charge of a ship's bridge at sea, states that when running in restricted visibility a ship will ". . . go at a moderate speed (safe speed today), having careful regard to the existing circumstances and conditions."

In 1956, moderate speed was defined as a ship's ability to stop within half the distance of the visibility. Any ship exceeding this speed limit can be held responsible for whatever happens. Consider the "existing circumstances and conditions" at Nantucket light ship who broadcast during the sinking, ". . . weather foggy-visibility fifteen yards." Under these circumstances and conditions the *Andrea Doria* should have been running at a speed no greater than her ability to stop within 22.5 feet! If every ship sailing the great circle route from ports on the eastern seaboard of the United States to or from ports in northern Europe abided by this dictate there would be a fleet of ships lying dead in the water for days at a time. There is not a ship of any size afloat that could stop in 22.5 feet from inching along as slow as the ship could possibly move. The fog off the Grand Banks, through which these ships must travel, is practically continuous especially during the month of July.

Although the *Stockholm* denied there was fog, the circumstantial evidence is conclusive that both ships were running faster than Rule #19 allowed. At the official inquiry Captain Calamai issued a statement that explained the problem of Rule #19 as far as a captain is concerned. He said that he was scheduled to arrive at Ambrose light ship, the entrance to New York, at 0700 on July 26, and that passing Nantucket light ship, 200 miles east of Ambrose light ship, he was running one hour late. Late arrivals cost ship owners and operators money. Any captain habitually tardy in his arrivals would soon be seeking a new job. The real culprits are not the captains or navigators but rather the owners/operators who force them to take calculated risk in order to stay on schedule.

The use of radar on shipboard brought forth lively reactions at conferences. The preliminary paragraph in that part of the Rules of the Road dealing with "Conduct in Restricted Visibility," states: "The possession of information obtained from radar does not relieve any vessel of the obligation of conforming strictly to the Rules, and, in particular, the obligations contained in Rule #35 (sounding of fog signals) and Rule #19 (speed in restricted visibility)."

It is a well known and seldom discussed fact that ships continually use radar as a form of navigation and aid to prevent collisions in restricted visibility. This procedure was defended time and time again at the conferences. When fog sets in, the usual procedure is to notify the captain who will come to the bridge. The engines are placed on "stand by" and the ship continues at full speed while fog signals are sounded at intervals of not more than two minutes.

The captain and watch officer then devote most of their attentions to the radar scope while lookouts posted on the bridge and bow listen for the fog signals of other ships. When a target appears on the radar scope a competent radar observer can determine the target's course, speed and closest point of approach in the matter of minutes. Then, if deemed necessary, collision avoidance action is taken. The general rule is whenever possible never to come closer to a radar target than two miles.

Those who expressed opinions were unanimous that the third officer, on the *Stockholm's* bridge, was not plotting the oncoming *Andrea Doria* by a radar that also had no gryo input. It was necessary to manually input the ship's true course. In fact many expressed doubt that the third officer even knew how to plot a radar target.

An interesting observation relative to the *Stockholm's* error in radar range concerned the third officer's own testimony. He said that just prior to leaving the wheelhouse for the chart room to obtain his 2300 RDF fix, he checked the radar screen and found it clear of any targets. Had the radar been operating on the fifteen mile range as he claimed, the *Andrea Doria* would have appeared on the *Stockholm's* radar screen at 2253, or seven minutes before the third officer left the wheelhouse at 2300.

Importance was placed on the fact that Carstens-Johannsen should have been well aware that his ship was apparently encountering fog. Weather reports containing information about conditions in this vital 200 mile span between Ambrose and Nantucket light ships were continuous and available. These, at least, should have aroused his curiosity enough to cause him to check the weather himself. Comments were also made that Captain Nordenson should have been on the *Stockholm's* bridge. Had he been there, he most surely would have had the engines placed on "stand by" with the customary fog signals being sounded periodically. By his own testimony, had this been the case, there would not have been a collision.

It was the third officer's responsibility to notify the captain when he felt conditions warranted placing the engines on "stand by" and actuating the fog signaling device. Apparently, it was thought, he was afraid he might provoke the captain's ire by causing him to leave his comfortable quarters and report to the bridge. The third officer simply continued to use the radar without plotting and claiming he had lookouts posted on the bridge and crow's nest with orders to "keep a sharp lookout for a ship on the port!"

The question of fog signals and lookouts was brought up. The *Stockholm* was not sounding fog signals, which obviously is the answer to the *Andrea Doria's* third officer's question: "Why don't we hear him? Why doesn't he whistle?"

In reverse, this question by the *Andrea Doria's* third officer has much greater significance. The *Stockholm* allegedly had lookouts posted on the bridge and crow's nest. According to the book <u>Collision Course</u>, the *Andrea Doria* was blasting her fog whistle every one hundred seconds. Under normal conditions, this giant fog whistle could be heard from two to five miles away – especially by anyone who should be intently listening for such signals. Nowhere is there evidence to indicate that the *Andrea Doria's* fog whistle was heard by the *Stockholm* until after the ships had sighted each other about one minute before the collision when the *Andrea Doria* sounded two blasts indicating she was turning left. Under the circumstances that existed that night one thing is certain – the *Andrea Doria's* fog signals should have been heard and reported at least five minutes before the collision.

Like the *Stockholm*, the *Andrea Doria* also used the radar as a form of navigation and aid to prevent collision. Unlike the *Stockholm*, the *Andrea Doria's* captain was on the bridge, her engines were on "stand by" and fog signals were being sounded at one hundred second intervals. And, like the *Stockholm*, the *Andrea Doria* was not plotting radar targets which Captain Calamai frankly admitted. Even had the *Andrea Doria* been plotting, the *Stockholm's* 22½° right turn into the collision which was executed during the final three minutes could not possibly have been recognized on the *Andrea Doria's* scope in time for collision avoidance action.

Comment was made that, like those on the *Stockholm*, the men on the *Andrea Doria's* bridge were not competent radar observers as far as plotting was concerned. This was further established by Captain Calamai's testimony. At least there were three officers on the *Andrea Doria's* bridge with one constantly monitoring the radar. In addition, the radar had a gyro repeater input. Radar came into its own during World War II when the Navy, with highly skilled personnel, used it to great advantage in naval warfare. Training and demonstrated competence in the use of the radar was not mandated in 1956.

The expressed intention of Captain Calamai, of the *Andrea Doria*, to pass the *Stockholm* to the starboard at a beam at a passing distance of one-half mile was criticized. This distance was much too close under any circumstances but even more so in considering the heavy fog the *Andrea Doria*, and surely the *Stockholm*, was encountering at the time.

* * *

It was felt that, no more than ten minutes after the *Andrea Doria* had picked up the *Stockholm* by radar twenty-six minutes before the collision when the ships were still ten miles apart, Captain Calamai should have ordered a substantial change in course to the right for two reasons. Primarily, to prepare for a left side-to-left side passing of the *Stockholm* at a distance of no less than two miles and secondly to indicate his actions and intentions on the *Stockholm's* radar screen. It was also noted that, although there were shoal waters in areas to the right of the *Andrea Doria's* course between Nantucket and Ambrose light ships, Captain Calamai's navigational charts would have shown him there was ample deep water in the immediate area for him to prepare for a left side-to-left side passing at a distance of two miles. Had the *Andrea Doria* acted according to this suggested rule of passing left side-to-left side, red light-to-to red light, the collision would not have happened. However, the increasing radar bearing of the *Stockholm* to the right assured Captain Calamai that he should maintain his course.

It was apparently the *Stockholm's* third officer's intention to pass the *Andrea Doria* wide in a left side-to-left side passing when he ordered the 22½° right turn three minutes before the collision. Unfortunately, the *Andrea Doria* was only two miles away when this substantial change in course to the right was ordered, not six miles which he must have believed. This confirms once again the *Stockholm's* error in radar range. Had the third officer ordered this 22½° right turn knowing the *Andrea Doria* was only two miles away would be to say that he intentionally caused the collision by turning directly into the *Andrea Doria*. No one has ever entertained such a thought.

*   *   *

Excessive speed in restricted visibility was mentioned. This violation of the Rules of the Road is so common that it received little attention. It was repeated many times that it is not what you do but rather what you are caught doing that is the problem.

*   *   *

HAD the *Stockholm's* engines been operating under "stand by" orders in accordance with Rule 19 instead of *"all clear full speed ahead"* the collision would not have happened.

Captain Nordenson testified that because of his high powered diesel engines, which were 100% efficient (horsepower wise) in the astern motion and which could be instantly reversed, the *Stockholm* could be stopped dead in the water from full speed ahead in the matter of one minute and 36 seconds and/or a distance of 1200 feet. This was the reason he gave for running at full speed in whatever restricted visibility he was willing to admit existed. This ability to stop, by the *Stockholm*, was probably accomplished at the ship's sea trials at the time she was built with all conditions at the optimum. It is clear from what happened in this disaster that conditions were far from optimum as far as the *Stockholm's* ability to stop was concerned.

At her speed of 18.5 knots, the *Stockholm* was advancing at the rate of some 1800 feet per minute. The emergency "full speed astern" ordered to stop the ship was issued at least one minute before the collision. The question is: If the *Stockholm* could have been stopped in a distance of 1200 feet and the emergency order to stop the ship was given when the ships were at least 1800 feet apart, why was the *Stockholm* still running fast enough to plunge half way through the *Andrea Doria* at nearly full speed?

The answer is elementary: For two vital reasons the *Stockholm's* engines were apparently <u>not</u> ready or prepared to respond to this emergency order. Had the engines been under "stand by" orders they would have been ready to respond instantly to any order issued from the bridge. Thus, at the very least, the *Stockholm* would have slowed down enough to allow the *Andrea Doria* to get safely across her bow.

The *"all clear full speed ahead"*, under which the *Stockholm's* engines were operating, required no engineering officers to be at or near the throttles controlling the engines. Thus, they could have been anywhere within the ship's cavernous engine rooms when the emergency order was given. Jostra Harald Svensson, the second engineer in charge of the engine room, testified that he happened to be standing on the maneuvering platform when the emergency order was given stating, "I immediately stopped both engines, then I started the starboard engine full astern. Next, I went to the controls of the port engines. I was about to start it when the collision happened and I was thrown forward ten or twelve feet."

Edwin S. Bjorkegren, the third engineer and second in charge, testified that he was in the auxiliary engine room when the emergency order was given. He continued that, he was still racing toward the maneuvering platform when the collision happened and he was also thrown forward.

By no means did the second engineer stop the engines when he placed the throttles in the "stop" position. All this did was to stop the fuel oil from being delivered to the engine's cylinders and did not stop the ship any more than one could stop an automobile by removing the foot from the gas pedal without applying the brakes. Forward momentum would keep the engines turning over at a fast pace while the ship gradually slowed down and eventually stopped. From the time lapse between placing the throttles in the "stop" position until the second engineer got the starboard engine started in the astern motion indicates there was no compressed air available to start the engines once they had been stopped. This would be comparable to a motorist attempting to start an automobile with a dead battery. Also, an automobile's engine turns only in one direction. To reverse a car's direction, the driver simply shifts gears. Such is not the case with motor ships where the engines are built to operate in either direction. After the throttle has been placed in the "stop" position, compressed air is also necessary to shift the engine's cam shaft to change the cylinder's firing cycle to operate the engine in the opposite direction. Had there been compressed air available at the maneuvering platforms, the *Stockholm's* engines could have been running at "full speed astern" in the matter of seconds.

Vital compressed air needed to maneuver the engines had always been secured when the engines were placed under "all clear full speed ahead" conditions. This is done by closing the valves at the compressed air storage tanks usually located in a remote part of the engine room. Thus, the very high air pressure on the pipe lines between the air tanks and the engines is relieved during the long ocean passage when this compressed air is not needed. When a "stand by" order is received the valves on the air storage tanks are opened after which engineers remain on the maneuvering platform ready to instantly respond to any order transmitted from the bridge. It appears that this procedure was also used on the *Stockholm* thus making it necessary for someone to open the valves on the compressed air storage tanks before anything, other than placing the throttles in the "stop" position, could be accomplished. From an engineer's point of view, the *Stockholm's* second engineer should be complimented for accomplishing as much as he did in the time made available to him. Had this been the case, Captain Nordenson's contention that his ship could be stopped in one minute and 56 seconds or 1200 feet would have been correct or nearly correct.

* * *

By contrast the *Andrea Doria*, a steam turbine driven ship, had poor reversing or backing power, a characteristic common to all turbine powered ships. As opposed to motor ships, a turbine driven engine revolves in one direction only. Therefore, it is necessary to have separate turbines for reversing purposes. These turbines, directly coupled to the propeller shafts by means of reduction gears, revolve in a vacuum when a ship is traveling ahead. For economic reasons and because there is little use for reversing power, these turbines are smaller and generate considerably less power than delivered by the ahead turbines. A turbine's efficiency is in velocity and many of these engines revolve as much as 5000 revolutions per minute. To stop, or reverse a ship's direction, the smaller turbines must first overcome this velocity before they can start to reverse the propeller's direction. With its lower power this is time consuming, thus a ship traveling at full speed would advance a couple of miles before stopping.

* * *

Both vessels were at excessive speed in fog. The *Andrea Doria* could be criticized for altering course to port from 269° to 265° at 2305 in violation of Rule 19(d)(i). *However,* the *Andrea Doria* was operating with engines on stand-by, fog signals were being sounded, the radar was being monitored and *the master was on the bridge.* On the *Stockholm,* her engines were <u>not</u> on stand-by, the fog signals were <u>not</u> being sounded, the radar was <u>not</u> being monitored properly, and *the master was not on the bridge*. As a result, the third officer made the fatal error by misusing his radar that resulted in bringing his vessel into a collision course in extremis. It would be impossible to stop his vessel to avoid impact. These facts, are in the author's opinion, the major reason for this maritime accident. Collisions at sea just don't happen, they are caused.

Although Captain Calamai's judgment was criticized by mariners, his absolute integrity was never questioned. By the same token, the *Stockholm's* third officer testimony was questioned in its entirety. As one participant said, "About the only truthful portion of the third officer's testimony was his admission that the *Stockholm* had been in collision with the *Andrea Doria*—a fact he could not very well deny!"

CHAPTER FIVE

MIRACULOUS RESCUE AND THE ANSWER TO WHY THE ANDREA DORIA SANK

With the *Andrea Doria* listing 20° to starboard shortly after the collision, rendering the port side lifeboats unavailable, there was a need for lifeboats. The largest rescue vessel with the most lifeboats was the Ile de France. The 53 year old captain, Raoul de Beaudéan with 1,767 persons on board was headed for France and presently 44 miles from the disaster scene. Captain de Beaudéan orders his crew to prepare to launch eleven lifeboats and turns his vessel around to head back for the rescue mission. Meanwhile, Nantucket Lightship reports "weather foggy—visibility 15 yards."

Aboard the *Stockholm*, Captain Harry Gunnar Nordenson makes his way to the bridge to find third officer Ernst Carstens-Johannsen bewildered and shaking. Demanding information, he learns that there's been a collision with another ship. He immediately orders the shutting of the watertight doors, which had already been done.

"Who is she?" Nordenson brusquely inquires, watching the wounded stranger disappear into the fog's anonymity. "I don't know," the watch officer responds, still perplexed and traumatized.

This second major shipping disaster in the 20th century did not result in the loss of life that occurred when the Titanic collided with an iceberg and resulted in the deaths of 1,522 passengers and crew mostly due to hypothermia. This collision between the *Stockholm* and the *Andrea Doria* resulted in the loss of 46 passengers and six crewmen. In contrast to the Titanic the rescue of the survivors of the *Andrea Doria* was the greatest rescue at sea in history. With the relative calm and warm waters there was no chance of hypothermia.

A great deal of credit for this rescue must be attributed to Captain Calamai, his officers and crew. In addition, a well designed and built vessel was able to withstand the impact of the *Stockholm's* ice-reinforced bow and its full ahead speed of 18.5 knots. To remain afloat until 10:00 am the next morning was indeed an attribute of a well built ship and allowed plenty of time for all the survivors to abandon it. There was enough time for all rescue vessels to rendezvous in the area and gather the following number of survivors onboard:

Ile de France	730
Stockholm	545
Cape Ann	168
Pvt. William H. Thomas	156
USCG Hornbeam	<u>45 mostly crew and Capt. Calamai</u>
Total	1,644 survivors

The number of survivors aboard each ship varies slightly according to different sources but there is no doubt that the Ile de France was the hero vessel having reversed course and headed back at full speed to arrive in time to rescue 730 people.

Immediately after the collision, Captain Calamai became a scapegoat for the collision as many believed his officers and crew did not behave in the best tradition of the sea during the rescue. Although this criticism was unjustified due mainly to prejudice and lack of evidence, unfortunately it still remains as the generalized thinking today of the uninformed public.

Why the *Andrea Doria* Sank

The appendix to the Italian Round Table discussions of October 6, 1988 stated that the *Andrea Doria* complied with the severe requirements of the Safety of Life at Sea (SOLAS) 1948 International Convention. SOLAS 48 established the number of compartments which can be flooded in relation to the characteristics of the ship. It also establishes the maximum list which the ship can reach at the end of the flooding or the "minor" list which does not submerge the margin line (a line parallel and close to the bulkhead deck line).

The *Andrea Doria* breach was more than 13m (+152%) longer than the "conventional breach, the penetration was 3.5m deeper (+64%), the height was higher than the conventional by a little less than 8m (+70%). Instead of remaining under the bulkhead deck (A deck) the penetration heavily damaged it and the foyer deck, and the upper deck finished with its edges just below the promenade deck. The area of the breach was 4.25 times larger than the standard breach defined in SOLAS 48.

The *Stockholm* acted as an inert mass provoking a severe chafing, accompanied by a deafening noise and sparks that seemed like fireworks, while inside there was smoke, acrid fumes and heat. This chafing caused deformation and tearing, its area included 150 portholes and about ten side ports. Two of these side ports (1st class foyer and storerooms) were, according to witnesses, caved in. The generator room filled in about one hour. The boiler and turbo-reduction gear rooms were abandoned after three hours due to the advanced state of the flooding from the upper starboard side. This was a case of what the English call "continuous flooding", that is, a multiple of different flows of water from the main breach, from the large broken pipes, from the lacerated hull, and the caved-in access ports and broken portholes.

The ship miraculously 'survived' for eleven hours, and sank with a list of almost 90°, less than the overturning angle. Contrary to that stated by many, the *Andrea Doria* did not capsize and, with its angle of inclination still less than 90°, she rested on the bottom, as confirmed by divers.

In their petition submitted to the Federal Court and throughout the lengthy inquiry, the *Stockholm's* owners maintained that the *Andrea Doria* capsized before she sank, not because of the collision, but because she was improperly ballasted and therefore not seaworthy. They contended that the lack of this proper ballasting affected the *Andrea Doria's* stability causing her to list beyond her maximum tolerance seconds after the collision. Then, as increasing sea water continued to pour into the stricken hull through uncontrolled flooding the list continued to increase until the ship finally rolled over on her beam ends before sinking. For this reason, the *Stockholm's* owners disclaimed any responsibility for the loss of the *Andrea Doria*.

Naval architects and marine engineers agree with this theory as the only reasonable explanation for the loss of the ship.

The board of experts who conducted the Congressional investigation at the same time the official inquiry was in progress also were inclined to agree with this ballast and stability theory.

In this Board's report, submitted to the Honorable Herbert C. Bonner, Chairman of the House Merchant Marine and Fisheries Committee, the experts wrote: "Briefly, the analysis shows that the *Andrea Doria* met the subdivision requirements of the 1948 Safety of Life at Sea Convention by a very narrow margin. It is stated in the 'stability report' that the ship could also meet the stability requirements of the

1948 convention provided she was kept ballasted with substantial and specified quantities of liquids in her various tanks. It does not appear possible to account for the behavior of the ship immediately following the collision on July 25, 1956, except on the assumption that she was not in fact ballasted in accordance with the information at that time.... And, finally, the fact remains that a fine, relatively new ship, built in accordance with the latest international convention, did sink."

Italian marine surveyor Maurizio Eliseo stated that the *Andrea Doria* met not only the SOLAS 48 requirement of a minimum metacentric height of 0.5 foot, but a higher requirement imposed by the Italian flag authorities of no less than 1.0 foot. When it sank, its matacentric height was more than 3.3 feet. The ballasting plan and record, saved by the engine crew, were among the papers sent to the court of New York for the crew's interrogation—which, unfortunately, never took place.

Had the *Andrea Doria* been ballasted properly, however, she would have remained in an upright position after the collision with full use of her facilities. In view of the fact that she remained afloat for about eleven hours after the collision, meant that she could have entered New York in an upright position despite the large hole in her side. If during this transit there were indications that she might not make it, Captain Calamai would had had the option of beaching the ship in shallow water never more than a few miles away.

As it was, the ever increasing list rendered the ship's rudder more and more useless. Instead of functioning to port or starboard it would not react in an up and down motion. The list caused the port side propeller to become ineffective as it rose to the surface. Captain Calamai recognized the futility of attempting to move his ship in any direction. Therefore, he sent out an urgent plea for tugs and ordered the two red lights run up on a signal halyard indicating that the *Andrea Doria* was now "not under control."

Figures 8 and 9 illustrate where and how the *Stockholm* penetrated the *Andrea Doria's* starboard side. In so doing, she broke open the five starboard side deep tanks and center line pipe tunnel, while the five port side tanks remained tight and empty. This permitted five hundred tons of sea water to affect instantly the ship's stability causing her to lean over to starboard more than twenty degrees in the first minute which was far beyond her maximum tolerance. Figure 10 displays an elevation view of the collision area.

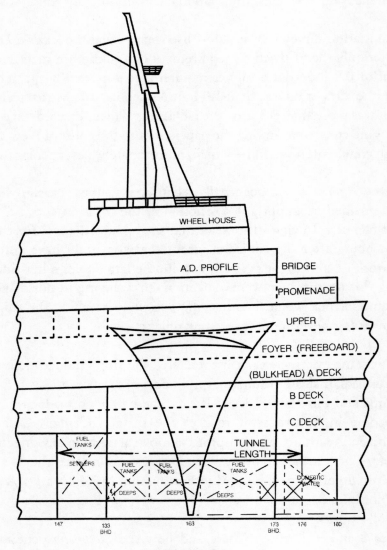

Figure 8A

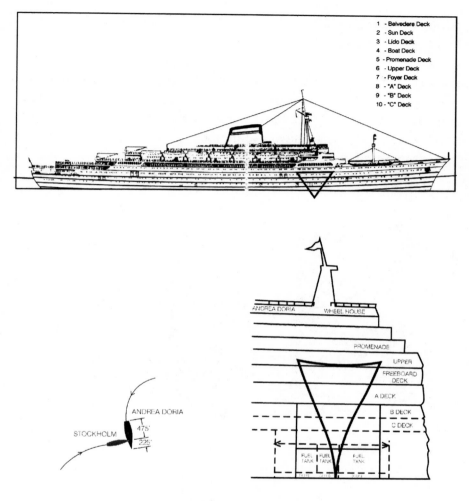

1	- Belvedere Deck
2	- Sun Deck
3	- Lido Deck
4	- Boat Deck
5	- Promenade Deck
6	- Upper Deck
7	- Foyer Deck
8	- "A" Deck
9	- "B" Deck
10	- "C" Deck

Figure 8B

Figure 8 (a and b). **Profile view of impact area.**

The fact that the center line pipe tunnel had also been breached by the collision made it impossible for the engineers to get at the valves controlling the port side deep tanks in an effort to counteract the ever increasing list to starboard. In addition, there was no watertight door between this pipe tunnel and generator room which was in the adjacent watertight compartment. Thus, the area outlined in Figure 9 also began to flood.

Naval architect Francesco Scotto responds to anyone who questions whether there was a missing door going to the water-tight compartments or whether these doors were closed: "The water-tight doors were closed perfectly at the moment in which the measures for navigating in fog were taken."

Figure 9A

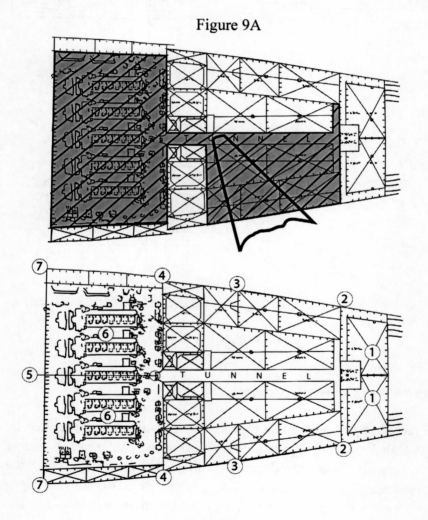

Figure 9B

Figure 9 (a and b). Overview of *Stockholm* penetration

9(a)   Illustrates *Stockholm's* penetration into *Andrea Doria*. Shaded area indicates area flooded as the result of this penetration.

○Circle: Missing water tight door between the pipe tunnel and generator room; a door about the size of a standard home type refrigerator door. Its presence would have had no bearing on the ultimate result as the ship listed beyond her maximum tolerance the moment she was hit and long before any appreciable amount of water had flooded into the generator room.

9(b)   Shows location of watertight bulkheads dividing the ship into separate watertight compartments up to the bulkhead deck. (See Figures 8(a and b)

#1   cargo hold #2
#2   watertight bulkhead, frame #173, between impact area and #2 hold impact area, breached deep tanks and pipe tunnel
#3   watertight bulkhead, frame #153 probably damaged
#4   generator room isolation bulkhead
#5   missing watertight door in isolation bulkhead
#6   generator room
#7   watertight bulkhead, frame #130 between generator and boiler room

The four fuel storage tanks between the generator room and the affected deep tanks apparently carried the fuel for the five diesel generators supplying electricity throughout the ship. These generators were secured one at a time as the water rose from the starboard side.

The *Andrea Doria* had many combination fuel oil storage and ballast deep tanks which required a liquid (fuel oil or sea water) ballast for sufficient weight to maintain stability. Some and perhaps all of these combination tanks were empty at the time of the collision. Most certainly the ten deep tanks in the affected area were empty. The reason these tanks were empty was because Captain Calamai knew that he had to be prepared to receive 2400 tons of fuel oil during the ship's short turn around in New York, where the ship was scheduled to dock the morning after the collision.

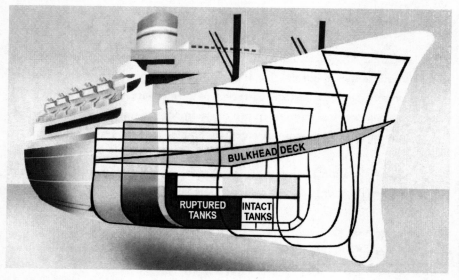

Figure 10. Collision area

Figures 8, 9 and 10: Courtesy of John Carrothers

Italian marine surveyor Maurizio Eliseo stated, "The ballasting record clearly confirms that the vessel still had 1,907 tons of fuel oil (more than sufficient to complete the return leg of its voyage); therefore, it didn't need to fuel in New York to be properly ballasted and safe, as has been suggested elsewhere. Yes, the *Doria's* fuel tanks were half empty at the time of the sinking, but it was built to return safety to Genova on the remaining fuel. This was demonstrated by the ship's previous 100 trips and those of its sister ship, the *Cristoforo Colombo.*"

Had Captain Calamai arrived at his berth in New York with these tanks filled with a mixture of sea water and the residue to fuel oil it is doubtful that he would have had sufficient time to dispose of this contaminated water, receive his fuel oil, and depart on schedule. Water mixed with the residue of fuel oil may not be pumped overboard in any harbor because of pollution. Therefore, the *Andrea Doria's* owners would have been obliged to resort to the very costly and time consuming process of hiring empty sludge barges with tugs to receive and take away this contaminated water for disposal before the fueling operation could start.

Another factor that must be considered regarding the water-tight compartments is that the two ships were traveling at high speeds: the *Stockholm* at its maximum 18.0 knots and the *Doria* at a slightly reduced speed of 21.8 knots. Additionally, the *Stockholm* hit the *Doria* just under the bridge wing with its steel-reinforced, ice-breaking bow. Because the *Stockholm* was riding lower than its target—being half its size—it had the effect of pushing the *Doria* to its left. In addition, since the *Doria* was speeding "hard to port" as ordered by its captain (in order to avoid the collision with the approaching *Stockholm* on its starboard side), this also caused it to lean onto its left side, further exposing the keel. Under these conditions, the keel became vulnerable to a blow from the *Stockholm*.

To further corroborate the damage, David Bright dove to the wreck in July 2006. This was his 121st dive to the *Andrea Doria*. He wanted to prove that the keel of the *Doria* was indeed breached and thereby doomed to sink. Concerning his previous dives, David stated: "Most divers use different mixes of oxygen, nitrogen and helium at different depths to prolong their dive time, reduce the disorientation from nitrogen narcosis and reduce the decompression time to remove the excess nitrogen from their bodies on the way back up so they won't get 'the bends'—decompression sickness that could be fatal. This non-dimensional environment can strike terror in the mind of an inexperienced diver; there're no point of reference except the dive line you're gripping and the air bubbles from divers below you. After several minutes, the light beam reflects upon the wreck at 170 feet down. It's eerie seeing the *Andrea Doria* where it was never meant to be. She's lying with her starboard side burying in the sand as if she wants to hide the mortal wound."

Today required technical gear includes a dry-suit, several underwater flashlights, diving reels, knives, a lift bag, and spare gas cylinders. The dry-suit will keep the body dry and warm since normal bottom temperatures are in the mid-40s Fahrenheit during the summer, even with a surface temperature of about 60° Fahrenheit. With the advent of new diving technologies, closed-circuit re-breathers are replacing scuba tanks as the preferred method for diving the *Doria*.

Before his last dive on Saturday, July 8, 2006, David Bright was quoted as saying, "Exploring the deep is as challenging as exploring another planet when dealing with air supply. At the depth of the *Doria*, pressure increases by about six or seven times; the partial pressures of gases increase to a point that the body cannot handle, and air becomes toxic. Nitrogen can have a menacing side effect. It can act as a narcotic and can severely impair one's abilities to dive safely. This is known as nitrogen narcosis or 'getting narced.' Sea explorer Jacques Cousteau called it 'raptures of the deep.'

David Bright did verify just prior to his last dive that the force of the collision did breach the keel of the *Andrea Doria*.

Shipwrecks are time capsules of human civilization. Underwater archaeology gives us the tools to rediscover mankind's moments that were forfeited before their rightful time—David A. Bright

As with the *Andrea Doria*, David Bright's life was forfeited before its rightful time.

CHAPTER SIX
THE OFFICIAL INQUIRY

Professional mariners, who followed the civil court proceedings in this case, were astounded by the testimony given under oath in the Federal Court of the United States by Ernst Carstens-Johannsen, the *Stockholm's* third officer who was in charge of her bridge at the time of the collision.

Amazement was compounded when, in cross examination, it was proved to this third officer that his testimony was "impossible and untrue." Faced with this irrefutable fact he simply changed the story he had written in his log book *at the time of the collision* to one that totally defied common sense.

As for the importance of the logbooks during the trial, a competent attorney with the opportunity to address this subject could easily demonstrate that entries in logbooks are made after completing the watch; hence, entries are subjective. Third officer Carstens-Johannsen produced his logbooks, but his alleged entries had been erased. On the other hand, Captain Calamai admitted to his crew's error in leaving the logbooks on board, but it must be considered that this was an oversight made under life-threatening conditions. Should the logbooks be an issue at all in a court of law? The logbook is written after the watch, not as an event happens. The fact that the logs were lost is not that relevant. I think the lawyers made this a bigger issue than it was. What is relevant is the information stored on the course recorder graph.

The only reasonable conclusion we have been able to reach from these proceedings in the Federal Court is that the case was settled between the owners of the two ships in order to hold their financial obligations to the third party claimants within the terms outlined in the Limitation of Liability. Thus, they were able to settle these claims for death and injury and the loss of personal effects and cargo amounting to $85 million for less than $6 million or for about seven cents on the dollar.

There is not the slightest doubt in our minds that had the court been fully informed of the facts and circumstances surrounding the happenings of that night, limitation of liability surely would have been denied. The court would have then decided on what would have been a fair and equitable settlement within the framework of the $85 million asked for by the third party claimants.

The motives of Eugene Underwood, who represented the *Andrea Doria* at the official inquiry, and Charles Haight, who represented the *Stockholm*, seem quite apparent. However, what about Leonard T. Matteson who represented many of the third party claimants during the civil court proceedings? After all it was he and Mr. Underwood who proved to the *Stockholm's* third officer that his testimony was "impossible and untrue."

Had either ship in this *Andrea Doria* tragedy been of United States registry, or had the accident happened within the territorial boundaries of the United States, there would have been a full U.S. Coast Guard inquiry before the case was placed before the Federal Court for judgment. The court would then have the benefit of the expert and unbiased findings of qualified men upon which to base a fair and equitable settlement for all concerned. It is unthinkable that any lawyer would permit his prime witness to give the same testimony before a Coast Guard Board of Inquiry that the *Stockholm's* third officer gave under oath in the Federal Court. For this reason, those of us who primary interest in maritime accidents is safety and education, have been advocating legislation that would extend these Coast Guard investigations to include all foreign ships using the facilities of our courts to settle their civil suits.

The first indication that all was not right came thirteen days after the disaster when <u>The New York Times</u> published the text of the Swedish American Line's petition presented to the Federal Court of the United States. With this petition the newspaper also published diagrams illustrating the opposing points of view. In effect, the petition and diagram declared the *Stockholm had turned away from and into the Andrea Doria at the same time.* Thus, the *Stockholm's* story became suspect. When one considers that the *Stockholm* plunged into the starboard side of the *Andrea Doria*, the *Stockholm's* claim that the *Andrea Doria's* port side light was visible at a distance of two miles cannot be reconciled. Following is an excerpt from this petition, the parts under question appear in CAPS.

"THE *ANDREA DORIA* CAME INTO SIGHT AT A DISTANCE OF ABOUT TWO MILES, AS CHECKED BY RADAR. SHE WAS WELL ON THE PORT BOW OF THE *STOCKHOLM* AND IN THE POSITION ANTICIPATED FROM OBSERVATIONS AND PLOTTING ON THE RADAR. THE *ANDREA DORIA* WAS SHOWING HER RED, OR PORT SIDE, LIGHT AND HER WHITE MASTHEAD LIGHTS WERE OPEN SO AS TO PASS AT A SAFE DISTANCE TO PORT OF THE *STOCKHOLM* . . . ALTHOUGH THE VESSELS WERE IN A POSITION TO PASS SAFELY PORT-TO-PORT, RED-TO-RED, THE *STOCKHOLM* WENT TO STARBOARD TO GIVE EVEN GREATER PASSING DISTANCE. THE *ANDREA DORIA* HOWEVER, SUDDENLY CLOSED OUT HER RED LIGHT, showed her green light and VEERED SHARPLY ACROSS THE BOW OF THE *STOCKHOLM*. The *Stockholm* immediately went hard right and full astern, but it was impossible to avoid collision and shortly thereafter the starboard side of the *Andrea Doria* and the bow of the *Stockholm* came into collision . . ."

The inquiry began on September 19, 1956, just eight weeks after the disaster. This was to be a fact finding exploration conducted prior to the trial which would determine accountability at a later date. No one sat in judgment and the witnesses testifying under oath were examined and cross examined by lawyers representing all interested parties. The inquiry was supervised by four special Masters in Chancery, working on a rotational basis. These special Masters, appointed by Federal Judge Lawrence E. Walsh were: Simon H. Rifkind, a former Federal Judge; Louis M. Loeb, President of the association of the Bar of the City of New York; Mark W. Maclay, an admiralty lawyer, and; Benjamin A. Matthews, President of the New York County Lawyers Association. The first witness to testify was Ernst Carstens-Johannsen, the 26-year-old third officer of the *Stockholm*, who was in charge of her bridge at the time of the collision.

The third officer's testimony was a detailed carbon copy of what had been written in the text of his company's petition. The testimony of this witness, as well as that of Captain Calamai, has already been given and illustrated.

In this respect, the question which has been asked many times is, in view of the fact that the *Stockholm* plunged headlong into the *Andrea Doria* at a point directly under her green starboard side light, how did anyone of the *Stockholm* see the *Andrea Doria's* red port side light when she was allegedly sighted three minutes before the collision or at any time thereafter?

A monumental factor in the *Stockholm's* overall defense hinged on the answer to the vital question of: WHAT TIME DID THE THIRD OFFICER ALTER THE SHIP'S COURSE TO COMPENSATE FOR DRIFT HE FOUND AS THE RESULT

OF THE 2300 RDF FIX?

OF THE 2300 RDF FIX? Under oath the third officer testified that he picked up the *Andrea Doria* by radar at a distance of twelve miles just as he ordered a slight change in course following his 2300 RDF fix. The *Stockholm's* course recorder graph shows a three degree change in course (92 to 95 degrees) was ordered at 2305, plus or minus seconds.

In cross examination the attorneys were quick to point out to the third officer that his testimony was "impossible and untrue." In effect they proved to him that at 2305, when he ordered the slight change in course to compensate for drift he found as the result of his 2300 RDF fix, the *Andrea Doria* was only four and not twelve miles away from the *Stockholm*!

Faced with this irrefutable fact, the third officer simply explained that the 2300 entry he made in the *Stockholm's* logbook at the time of the accident should have been "about 2300." Furthermore, Carstens-Johannsen testified under oath that the steering of the helmsman was erratic and unreliable: "He is more interested in the surrounding things than the compass." This gave Mr. Underwood the opportunity to demonstrate, by producing the course recorder graph of the *Stockholm* as evidence, the significance of the wavering helm:

Q: Inasmuch as your ship was yawing 3 or 4 or 5 degrees and the bearing was a very fine bearing, it was of the utmost importance to be certain about your observations, was it not?

A: Yes.

Q: But you did not look at the compass, you asked the helmsman what the heading was, is that right?

A: If I had left the radar, he may have gone away from 91, so I had to rely upon the helmsman in a case like this.

Q: With your ship equipped as it was, that is, having no repeater, you had no alternative but to rely on the wheelsman, did you?

A: Yes.

Q: And if the helmsman is in error by one degree, that may throw off your bearing by as much as 50%, may it not?

A: Yes.

As the third officer found himself in a bind, he claimed that the Sperry course recorder expert, who had identified the change in the course at 11:05 PM (2305), was wrong. In spite of the self-contradictions and resulting uncertainties, the attorneys never re-addressed these issues; the contradictions were never officially established.

The third officer's denial of the 2305 change in course placed him in an untenable position. Now it was necessary to revert to the last previous slight change in course at 2240 (obviously made as the result of drift found in his 2230 RDF fix) at the time he picked up the *Andrea Doria* by radar at a distance of twelve miles. After informing his readers of this in Collision Course, Alvin Moscow continued that by calculations the "about 2300 RDF fix was actually taken at 2248. It was as the result of drift found at 2248, writes Mr. Moscow, that the third officer altered course at 2240. Neither of these contentions is acceptable. At 2240 the ships were 20.66 miles and not twelve miles apart. How could the third officer alter course at 2240 to compensate for drift he did not know existed until eight minutes later at 2248?

In 1959, when this information was found in Collision Course, a thorough search was made through John Carrother's file of newspaper clippings. The search failed to reveal anything other than the third officer's change in time from 2300 to "about 2300." While writing the book Mr. Moscow had, among other things, full access to the complete transcript of the official inquiry's testimony. Therefore, it must be assumed that this is where he obtained this information.

By the same token it must be assumed that the following alleged facts, taken from <u>Collision Course</u>, also came from the transcript of the testimony and are, as Mr. Moscow declared in his book, "factual and true." These alleged facts were presented by Mr. Moscow as proof that the third officer's testimony "correlated closely" with the *Stockholm's* course recorder graph. They cover the last hour before the collision and are presented in chronological order so that the sequence of events may be better understood.

#1   At 2210, the third officer altered course from a compass heading of 87 to 89 degrees to compensate for drift found twenty minutes later as the result of his 2230 RDF fix.

#2   The third officer picked up the *Andrea Doria* by radar at a distance twelve miles just as he ordered a slight change in course from a compass heading of 89 to 91 degrees at 2240 to correct for drift found eight minutes later as the result of his 2248 RDF fix which he thought was "about 2300." (note: at 2240, the ships were 20.66 miles apart.)

#3   The third officer waited for three minutes, until the distance between the ships had been reduced to ten miles before starting to plot the on-coming *Andrea Doria* by radar.

In order to correlate the *Andrea Doria's* actions with the foregoing while recognizing that the *Stockholm* was running at a speed of 18.5 knots, we find that it would have been necessary for the *Andrea Doria* to have increased her speed to 194.72 knots in order to reduce the distance between the ships from 20.66 to ten miles in three minutes. The *Andrea Doria* would then have resumed her normal speed of 21.85 knots when the third officer allegedly started his plotting procedure.

#4   The third officer then plotted the oncoming *Andrea Doria* at the regular and prescribed intervals until, three minutes before the collision, the *Andrea Doria* finally exposed herself from out of the fog right at the spot where his radar plotting told him she would appear.

The *Stockholm's* story for the final hour illustrated in Table 1 has already been covered in detail. Of interest to this author is the fact that seamen are creatures of habit. Watch officers normally fix their vessel's position at regular intervals (i.e. every six minutes ($1/10^{th}$ of hour) in confined waters, every 20 minutes ($1/3^{rd}$ of an hour) in less confined waters or in the case of the *Stockholm*, every thirty minutes (1/2 hour) in safer waters. Recording fixes at these intervals makes it easier to compute ship's speed and to determine the vessels set and drift. The third officer took three RDF fixes at 2200, 2230, and 2300. After the 2300 fix he saw the pip of the *Andrea Doria* for the *first time* at what he thought was a range of twelve miles. The real range was four miles. Shortly thereafter he executed the starboard course change based on scanty radar information that ended in disaster. Furthermore, in this author's opinion, the third officer *never* saw the *Andrea Doria's* port (red) side light. The only side light he saw was the *Doria's* starboard (green) side light when he was in extremis. It appears during the inquiry no one questions Carstens-Johannsen on his frequency of fixes. It is also obvious that the course change at 2305 was not a yaw but to compensate for his 2300 RDF fix. Finally no watch officer at sea would make a log entry as being *about* 2300.

With respect to this final three minutes no exception is taken with what Alvin Moscow has written. All newspaper accounts of this portion of the testimony have essentially told the same story.

Another questionable piece of information told in <u>Collision Course</u> concerns the course recorder graph and the third officer's entry in the *Stockholm's* logbook. Here Mr. Moscow has changed the graph's time by two minutes, from 2311 to 2309 to correlate the graph with the 2309 time of collision as noted in the logbook.

The disturbing part of this change in time is that on December 4, 1956, Russell Porter reported in <u>The New York Times</u> that Captain Nordenson, commanding officer of the *Stockholm*, had testified that with respect to the time of collision the third officer was in error. The accident happened at 2311, he said, as indicated by the graph and not at 2309 as erroneously noted in the logbook by the third officer. In other words, the captain said there was no difference between the ship's clock and the course recording instrument.

The official inquiry continued in this confused right-to-right or left-to-left atmosphere when, on January 24, 1957, more than four months after it began, the inquiry was suddenly terminated before many of the witnesses had been examined.

At the official inquiry it was proved to the *Stockholm's* third officer that portions of his testimony were "... impossible and untrue." Faced with this irrefutable fact he simply changed his story to one that was equally "impossible and untrue."

In their petitions addressed to the Federal Court, each ship blamed the other for the tragedy and asked the court for, as the *Stockholm's* lawyers phrased it: "... Exoneration From or Limitation of Liability, Civil and Maritime ..."

It is also reasonable to believe that the lawyers representing both defendants knew that their clients never would be exonerated. Therefore, they would aim for the next best settlement of their cases with the third party claimants for death and injury and the loss of personal effects and cargo—Limitation of Liability.

Limitation of Liability as applied in American Admiralty Law dictates that a steamship company cannot be held liable for any amount greater than the actual cash value of its ship after an accident. If the ship is a total loss the owner's financial liability is held to the sum of the revenue the ship was earning on her final voyage plus sixty dollars per gross ton of the ship if death and/or personal injury were involved. Under these circumstances the *Stockholm's* financial obligation could not exceed $4 million and the *Andrea Doria's* not more than $2 million. Third party claims against both defendants totaled $85 million.

There is one stipulation contained in the terms of Limitation of Liability that presents grave concern to the legal advisors of steamship companies. This provision states that if the court decided that a ship's owner had privy and knowledge of defects in seaworthiness or negligence in the operation of its ship—Limitation of Liability could automatically be denied.

This was an unusual case. There were two separate and isolated issues that should have been resolved before final judgment was made by the court. The first was the navigational blunder by the *Stockholm*. The second was why the *Andrea Doria* which should have survived the accident, capsized and sank.

As the official inquiry progressed it became apparent that the *Andrea Doria* was lost because she had been operating with a calculated risk. Since Captain Calamai obviously took this calculated risk with his owners' knowledge and consent, Limitation of Liability would, no doubt, have been placed in jeopardy. For this reason, we believe, his owners offered no defense for the actions that Captain Calamai took on the night of the collision. We also believe that this is the reason why Captain Calamai's owners and lawyers offered him nothing but a token defense against the *Stockholm's* perjury.

The *Stockholm's* legal advisors must have felt that the circumstantial evidence would refute the third officer's claim that the night was clear and he was justified in running at full speed without sounding fog signals. The third officer was compelled to make this claim because the *Stockholm's* engines under his control were operating under "all clear full speed ahead" orders. In restricted visibility a ship's engines should operate under "stand by" conditions thus she would be prepared to maneuver instantly. From the testimony of Captain Nordenson, the *Stockholm's* commanding officer, it can be proven that had the *Stockholm's* engines been on "stand by" when the emergency "full speed astern" order was rung up on the engine order telegraphs (EOT) about one minute before the crash, the collision would not have happened; because the *Stockholm*, at the very least, would have been slowed down enough to allow the *Andrea Doria* to get safely across the *Stockholm's* bow. From the severity of the collision it is apparent that little, if any headway had been taken off the *Stockholm* when she plunged half way through the *Andrea Doria*. All of this must have indicated to the *Stockholm's* counselors that they would be faced with culpable negligence on the part of the *Stockholm's* third officer and their chances for Limitation of Liability might well have been nullified.

As has already been noted, the entire official inquiry ran in a contradictory right-to-right and left-to-left vein. It was still running in full force when the inquiry suddenly terminated before several important witnesses had fully testified.

Apparently, both sides now felt they had confused the issues enough so that they could convince the Federal Court that the true answer could never be found. They requested the Court's permission to assume equal responsibility and to settle the third party claims within the terms of Limitation of Liability. The Court agreed and the claimants were forced to settle their claims amounting to a potential $85 million for less than $6 million, or about seven cents on the dollar.

Also waiting in the Court's docket were the counter suits filed by the steamship companies. The Swedish American Line, owners of the *Stockholm* had a claim pending in the amount of $2 million against the *Andrea Doria's* owners to pay for their ship's new bow and the loss of revenue while the ship was out of service. The Italian Line had countered with a suit in the amount of $30 million for the loss of the *Andrea Doria*.

In view of the out of court settlement of the third party claims, the two steamship companies dropped their counter suits. The forthcoming trial to start on April 1, 1957, to determine degree of responsibility, scheduled by Federal Judge Irving R. Kaufman, was cancelled. As far as the Federal Court was concerned, the *Andrea Doria-Stockholm* case became a closed book.

Forty years after the collision the testimony during the inquiry furnished raw material in order to reconstruct the collision and display the approach of both vessels on a computer driven simulator. The bridge simulator at the U.S. Merchant Marine Academy, in Kings Point, NY, is called CAORF, which stands for "computer assisted operational research facility." CAORF's components are displayed in Figure 11.

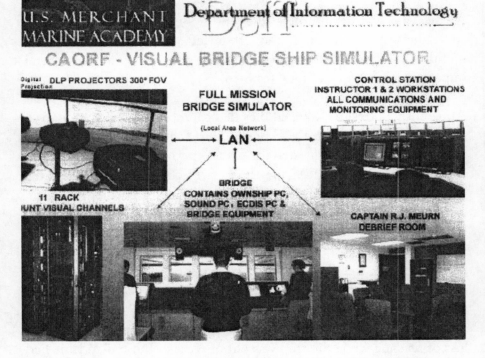

Figure 11. CAORF's Components (Computer Assisted Operations Research Facility at USMMA, Kings Point NY). Courtesy of Marilyn Hetsel, Director of Simulation

CAORF is designed for training and research, which will help to prevent accidents like the *Stockholm-Andrea Doria* collision and the grounding of the Exxon Valdez. By altering the visual field, academy cadets experience what it is like to be on the bridge watch ... thereby enhancing the third mate's decision-making skills as they apply to traffic and voyage planning situations.

Referring to the benefits of the simulator in explaining the *Stockholm-Doria* collision, we can put to the test human memory as challenged and explained via nautical science. The collision can be dissected and pieced back together, entertaining various scenarios and their viability. We are not at the mercy of the testimony alone.

In fact, testimony can be traced on computer screen to display every aspect. Then experts analyze whether the subjective words given under oath match the objective analyses of the computer. Using this lengthy scientific process, many conclusions about the *Andrea Doria-Stockholm* collision are evident and coincided with those of the Round Table discussed in the next chapter. Ten primary findings are:

#1   There is much to be said about the composition of the watch aboard the *Stockholm* (only one officer and three seamen), the quality (experience, capacity for thought) of the only officer on the bridge and the training of the three seamen and their experience. In particular, we refer to the helmsman, Larsen, only six months with the Swedish American Lines, who caused the yawing of several degrees to port and starboard of the course, with serious detriment to the direction finding capability on the radar.

#2   The lack of a LORAN type hyperbolic navigation system on the *Stockholm* led to uncertainty regarding the position of the ship. In fact, the person who handed over the watch to Carstens-Johannsen expressed this uncertainty, aggravated by the fact that he was unable to take the azimuth of the sun at sunset because it was covered by cloud. This brings us to ask: was it cloud or fog?

#3   Carstens-Johannsen then started to establish the ship's position, utilizing precious minutes for the radio direction finding measurements which, furthermore, being carried out at night, were affected by errors aggravated by the unsteady course. Moreover, this meant that he had to continuously move from the chart room to the bridge, with the consequent difficulty in concentrating on his primary watch duties.

#4   Neither Carstens-Johannsen nor the lookout heard the fog signal of the *Andrea Doria*. This would have indicated that the *Andrea Doria* was only two miles away not six. The whistle is certainly audible within two miles. If they had heard it, they would have been obliged to stop and proceed slowly (with a fog signal forward of the beam). This leads to the hypothesis that the bridge of the *Stockholm* was excessively noisy.

#5   Carstens-Johannsen declared to be puzzled at not seeing the lights of the *Andrea Doria*, when the distance would have allowed this in clear weather. The Official Bulletin issued by the Nantucket, submitted to the NY Court, at 1940 on July 25, stated fog with a maximum visibility of twenty-five yards.

#6   The telephone call from the *Stockholm's* lookout in the crow's nest compelled Carstens-Johannsen, the only officer on watch to answer, facing the stern at the moment, when all his attention should have been on the approaching *Andrea Doria*. It was 2310, sixty seconds before the collision, objectively already too late for any decisions.

#7   It appears that third officer, Carstens-Johannsen, definitely erred in the reading of his radar, especially the range of the *Andrea Doria*.

#8   The helmsman's yawing caused inaccuracy in the radar reading by the third officer. When Carstens-Johannsen first observed the radar pip of the *Andrea Doria* showed itself to the left of the heading flasher on *Stockholm's* radar. Based on this scanty radar information, the young third officer assumed port-to-port passage. In fact, it was the yaw to starboard by the *Stockholm's* helmsman that caused this appearance. The *Stockholm's* helmsman was obviously not a good steersman and his yawing was evident on the *Stockholm's* course recorder graph. This misread of the radar of the pip and being on the wrong range scale caused Carstens-Johannsen to drastically alter the *Stockholm's* course to starboard.

#9   Carstens-Johannsen claim that he saw a red port light at two miles distance is not viable. We found that at no time could Carstens-Johannsen nor the lookout have seen the *Andrea Doria's* red/port sidelight during the approach of the two vessels.

#10   If the third officer heard the fog whistle, as he stated, he should have known there were fog conditions . . .and in accordance with Rule #19 should have put the ship on stand-by conditions, slowed his speed, and have a motorman at the throttle. Instead, one motorman was working three decks away from the throttle. When the *Doria* was sighted (from the bridge of the *Stockholm*, thirty seconds before the collision), and the throttle was finally placed on "full astern" (reverse), it was too late as the vessels were now in extremis.

In the final analysis, the CAORF simulator research coincided with the Round Table discussion and the *Andrea Doria* contention in Figure 1 on how the vessels reached their collision point. It was the only possible outcome when analyzing the course recorder graphs and the testimony from the official inquiry.

CHAPTER SEVEN

ROUND TABLE DISCUSSIONS

I n 1988 the Round Table published a report on the *Andrea Doria-Stockholm* collision. The group was composed of the *Andrea Doria's* officers, crew members, and officials with the Italian Lines. In addition, there were journalists, marine engineers, professors, navigation and radar experts.

The Round Table discussions were divided into five parts:

1.   What took place on the bridge prior to the collision, explained by Captain Giannini, who was Third Officer of the watch that night on the bridge.

2.   What took place in the engine room following the collision, explained by Chief Engineer Cordera, as Third Engineer at the time.

3.   What occurred on the bridge after the collision, explained by Captain Badano, who was Second Deck Officer.

4.   How the negotiations proceeded between the Underwriters and the shipping companies according to Dr. A. Boglione, a maritime lawyer and free lance professional man extraneous to the facts described herein.

5.   How the vessel behaved after the collision from the technical viewpoint.

All the studies have been verified by illustrious professionals and/or university professors. The texts have been approved by the group as a whole and do not, therefore, express personal opinions.

Of the 1,622 pages of the report, the report of the officer on watch aboard the *Andrea Doria* is most appropriate in discussion of the collision. What follows is a segment of the report of Eugenio Giannini, third officer on watch during the last hour until the collision, followed by Guido Badano's report.

Guido Badano's segment of his report takes us from 0300 in the morning of July 26, 1956, until the sinking of the *Andrea Doria*. He spent all of that time with Captain Calamai. There was a great mutual respect between the two officers. They shared their sadness and grief as both watched their beloved *Andrea Doria* sink shortly after 1000 (10:00 AM).

Captain Eugenio Giannini, Third Officer on Watch

At 22.20 *Andrea Doria* passes abeam of Nantucket, one mile to South. She swings to true course 269° the only direct course which may lead us to the Ambrose lightship to take on the pilot for arrival at New York. Our speed is 21.8 knots.

At 22.45 Franchini, the Deck Officer acting as radar-man, observes an echo on the radar screen 4° to starboard, at 17 miles distance, I am behind Franchini and have the possibility to verify these data. Later bearings recorded directly on the screen, assure us the target observed is a ship proceeding at the speed of 18 knots, on a course approximately parallel and opposite to our own; it ought to pass at about one mile abeam of our starboard. The echo of the ship under observation is continuously followed by Franchini, and the observations are reported to the Master who, every so often, personally verifies the situation.

There is concentration on *Doria*'s bridge, without tension. At 23.05 so as not to reduce the distance of the passage abeam, now imminent, Master Calamai orders to steer 4° to port, to 265°. At the time of this turn, "*Stockholm*" was about 3.5 miles distant.

At 23.09, *Andrea Doria* plots the echo at little more than one mile away, approximately 30° to starboard. Now the course of the other ship seems such as to reduce passage abeam to 9/10th of a mile, but 1668 metres are still a considerable and reassuring distance.

Now we can sight the glow of the approaching vessel and a few seconds later we are able to clearly raise the two white range lights: the lower one well to the right of the upper one. Also Master Calamai has sighted them. I am watching the and, in my binoculars, with astonishment. I see that she is rapidly hauling to starboard!

"She's bearing down on us", I shout. "She's coming right at us!" But the Master had already appraised the situation: too late to swing to starboard. Collision was by now inevitable! We try to escape: "Hard a-port!" We signal our turn with ship's whistles. Franchini asks: "Captain: what about the engines?" He replies, "No! Let them be! We need all the speed we've got now!" *Stockholm* was, by now, coming full at us, right into us without a signal. *Andrea Doria* is beginning to respond to the helm, but it's too late!"

Little more than a minute had passed, yet it seemed an eternity!

Stockholm rammed us right under the bridge crushing more than 20 metres of her stiffened bow into our hull. She slid along the full length of our starboard Side and thence to pass astern off starboard quarter. The handling of *Andrea Doria*, as may be observed from the course recorder, was unexceptionable. Never, I repeat, never from the moment of sighting on radar to that of the collision, was the *Stockholm* ever to port of our course or of our bow; never! But let us listen now to what was said by Swedish Officer Carstens. We take it from the testimony given at the preliminary hearing which took place in New York and quoted by Alvin Moscow, in his book entitled Collision Course, an author certainly not favorable towards us.

At 20.30, Carstens relieves Second Officer Enestrom on watch. Master Nordenson is in his quarters. The course is 90°. There is uncertainty as to the vessel's position. Enestrom deems the vessel to be 1.5 miles further to north than expected. At approximately 21.00 hours, Master Nordenson goes up on the bridge. Carstens enters the chartroom to determine the fix; using R.D.F. He takes two bearings. At 21.20 the Master enters the chartroom, looks at the chart and tells Carstens to order the helmsman to steer 97°. Evidently he wishes to pass nearer to the Nantucket lightship than he usually does; keep it north at not less than one mile, at not more than two.

At 21.45, the Master returns to his quarters telling Carstens to call him when Nantucket is raised. Carstens re-enters the chartroom and using D/F he takes bearing of Nantucket and Block Island signals; plots them on the chart; evaluates the position which is 2.5 miles north of the envisaged course. At 22.30 Carstens again determinates his vessel's position. What concerns him at the moment is that *Stockholm*, notwithstanding the degrees of correction, is increasingly more to the north of her pre-established course. He deems that the current is causing his vessel to drift further to the north. But his evaluation is incorrect, inasmuch as the current in that zone is insignificant and, in fact, the *Andrea Doria* was not affected by it. Moreover, it is to be noticed from the tide tables and from the excellent U.S. Coast Guard charts. The current, which shifted the vessel to north, had surely made itself felt prior to the vessel fixes of 21.00 and later.

At 22.04 she was 2.5 miles north, at 22.30 she was 2.7 miles north and Carstens orders a course change to 089°. At 22.48, Carstens, with three radio bearings, finds he is three miles to north of his estimated course. He is sure of this last fix and, therefore, orders to change course two more degrees to starboard to 91°. Shortly after, on his radar screen, he observes the echo of a craft: a weak signal, at 12 miles distance and, as he declares and confirms, slightly to port of his bow.

It's 23.00. At 23.05, whilst asking helmsman Larsen to give him the bearing of *Stockholm's* bow, he sees the target ten miles off, 2° to port. But, he adds, he is not sure of his bearings.

As it is to be seen, each bearing and every consequent decision is subordinate to the behavior of the helmsman who, we are aware, is a very poor helmsman.

At 23.07 he sights the target at six miles distance. Two things astonish Carstens: (1) The speed of the approaching vessel; (2) the fact that he is unable to see the vessel's lights with the naked eye. Not for one moment does the thought pass his mind that just a little ahead there be a bank of fog.

At 23.08, Biorkman, the bridge lookout, shouts: "Lights to port!" They will later declare having seen *Andrea Doria's* port red side light at 2 miles distance. Anticipating a port to port passage on opposite course, red to red, at less than one mile, Carstens orders a starboard swing of 2 points, 22½°. Carstens returns to the bridge to answer the phone; it's the crow's nest lookout who warns him, "Lights 20° to port." In order to make this phone call Carstens must cross the entire bridge and turn his back on the bow; thus, he loses sight of the bow.

At 23.10 having terminated his phone call, he sees that the situation has changed, so he affirms; from the port-side bridge-wing he sees a great illuminated ship which is crossing the *Stockholm's* course. He orders: "full speed astern— hard a-starboard!" Then the collision.

For thirty-two years now the mystery of the *Andrea Doria* has been the topic of discussion. I should say rather that this had been the mystery of the vessel *Stockholm*.

1.   Why does Carstens-Johannsen sustain that night was serene without fog when the Nantucket lightship meteo-bulletins are issued warning mariners of thick fog with visibility of less than 25 yards?

2.   Why does Carstens-Johannsen affirm to have plotted us always to port of his vessel—when I have demonstrated to you, utilizing his own testimony, that we have always been to starboard of his vessel?

3.   Why did he turn 22° to starboard when without changing course he would have passed abeam at a distance of one mile?

4.   Why did he order full to starboard, when he affirms having seen us pass before his bow? Had it been so, would a full turn to port have sufficed.

5.   Why does he sustain having plotted us a 23.06 at 1.9 miles to port, when collision occurred at 23.11 hours at a point which shows the impossibility of the 23.06 position of our ship?

6.   Why did someone—never will we know who—erase the plotting from the table on which Carstens-Johannsen affirmed to have performed same?

7.   Why did also the rough sea log mysteriously disappear from *Stockholm's* bridge? Why did Alvin Moscow, in his book,

<u>Collision Course</u> which some have considered a short of bible of the events, many times change the testimony given by third deck officer Carstens-Johannsen to correlate his reconstruction favorable to *Stockholm*?

8.   In this same book on page 48, 7th edition in English, from line 9 to 18, Carstens-Johannsen statement changes time by as much as twelve minutes. Why did Alvin Moscow not cite vital testimonies which could have proved prejudicial for *Stockholm*?

9.   Concluding as to why, once the controversy had been settled, did some authoritative voice not make itself heard to firmly answer these questions and to inform the public? Why, and why again?

I now think the evidence is such and so abounding that one may be astonished that after 32 years there may still be someone to convince. Ladies and gentlemen, I thank you for your attention and would conclude reminding you that the preliminary hearing in New York was suddenly closed due to the agreement reached between the opposing parties and thus not even all the witnesses called were heard. That is to say, the two shipping companies allowed the respective lawsuits, commenced one against the other, to lapse thus closing the case without deciding which of the ships had made an erroneous maneuver. But, notwithstanding that compromise, the victims of that night will ever weigh upon our conscience.

Captain Guido Badan, Second Deck Officer

The time is 03.00 hours. Engine room has been evacuated an hour ago. Only the emergency dynamo is still working. Four hours after the collision, the evacuation of the vessel is reaching completion and this is confirmed by the inspections made of all accessible spaces from which reports are received.

At approximately 04.00 hours, the Master dictates a message to be transmitted to the Company in Genoa and in New York, "Run down in thick fog by Swedish ship. Passengers transferred to rescue ships. Vessel in danger. Calamai." I take it to the wireless station adding the word "*Stockholm*". List is 35°. I once again check the closing of watertight doors by the red warning lights which are all alight on the bridge panel.

Then the bridge is reached by Kirn, Magagnini, Giannini, Donato, etc. Magagnini confirms to Master that all passengers have been disembarked and the negative outcome of the accommodation inspections. The Master is informed, at this moment, of the decease of Mrs. Peterson and another class passenger. Mr. Peterson and an officer from vessel *Smeralda*, a passenger of ours, who helped in the rescue operations, are the last two passengers to disembark as far as we are aware.

It is about 04.30-04.40 hours, (5½ hours after the collision). It is almost impossible to move around because of the heavy list reached. Using a handkerchief I bandage a grazed toe for Magagnini. Master gives the "Abandon ship!" order to all those who have remained on board with the exception of the ship's officers and some volunteers. Vessel *Ile de France* is freed and we thank her. (I thought all passengers were off now, who are these volunteers?)

The staff captain, acting also as our spokesman, advises the Master to transfer, all of us, to a lifeboat and to remain nearby, the same lifeboat with which our engine-room colleagues, who disembarked aft, are reaching us amidships. The Master declines by then accepts to go down to the boat deck. List is now approximately 40° which makes it difficult even to sit on the flooring.

With reference to the decision to abandon ship, I would transcribe here an excerpt from the report made by Captain Calamai upon arrival at New York. "With the absolute certainty that no passengers were still on board, the vessel having reached such a list that to remain longer would have meant nothing else but a useless sacrifice of human lives, the Chief Engineer having already confirmed to me that nothing more could be done inasmuch as only emergency dynamic and pump were still working, having consulted the staff captain and the officers present, I gave the oder to embark on the last boat. We left the vessel in order of rank. When the last officer had left the vessel, I too embarked." What Calamai does not report is that when Magagnini invites him to come away, he says quietly, with decision but almost bashfully, "You may go, I'm staying." I then understand the significance of a message to his daughters which Captain Calamai had whispered a few hours earlier and specifically after the arrival of *Ile de France*.

To continue the story of events: Magagnini returns on board, we refuse to leave them alone, and the Master allows himself to be persuaded. Lifeboat 11, approximately 05.30 hours.

I take up my position at the rudder tiller of the lifeboat into which we have transferred the Aldis flash-light searchlight, binoculars and megaphones; I stay there until the end. Following the instructions received he remains in the immediate vicinity of *Andrea Doria*. We transfer the confused and more fatigued persons to another boat. A U.S. warship passes us coffee, cigarettes and medicinals. *Ile de France*, having recovered her boats, salutes us with three blasts of her whistles and moves off. Aircraft of the press are flying over our heads. The tugs arrive and our Master goes on board the first tug to confer with that unit's master. During that talk, I watch the progressive list of the vessel until she sinks at 10.10 hours. Soon afterwards we are taken on board by the U.S. escort-destroyer *Allen* by which we arrive at New York at about midnight.

I agree with friend Cordera as to the great value of the work done by the engine-room personnal to whom I wish to express here the thanks of all the survivors; contrarily to my friend Cordera who, I recall, did also everything in his power to assist in the rescue of certain timid lady passengers in the fore zone struck by *Stockholm's* bow. I have cited names of persons to which I would add many others such as: Pazzaglia, Mantero, Ravasio, Pertini, ship's secretary Corosu, first sick-bay attendant Coretti, children's nurse Tartarini, boatswain's mate Serpe. Certificated seaman Pinelli, seaman Danesi, youngster Ignaro, waiter Rovelli and boy LaMotta on his first sea voyage, etc. all of them persons who went beyond their utmost and duty, who are able to complete and confirm this testimony which is too short for so vast a subject and who I am happy to remember united in the great anguish of the loss of so fine a vessel and in the sadness in which her Master had been abandoned.

Today, there is still a sadness in Guido Badano's voice as he reminisces about the loss of the *Andrea Doria*. He has stated on documentaries and to the author personally as he watched the *Andrea Doria* sink, "It is like watching a close friend die, a young one."

CHAPTER EIGHT

AFTERMATH

The *Andrea Doria* remains in her watery grave off Nantucket while *M/V Stockholm* still sails today under Cyprus flag as the Portuguese cruise ship *Athena*. In 1959, the *Stockholm* with her new one million dollar bow was sold to East Germany and sailed as the *Voiker Freund Schaft*. In 1986 she sailed as a cruise ship under Panamanian flag. After a brief period as a barracks ship in Oslo, Norway, she was sold to Italian interests.

In 1990, Italian papers greeted the liner with headlines that screamed *"e arrivata la nave della morte"* – the ship of death has arrived. Under ownership of Nina Cruises, she was renamed the *Italia Prima* and was rebuilt from the hull up emerging with a radically altered profile. The *Italia Prima* was outfitted at the same berth that the *Andrea Doria* departed from on her last voyage in 1956. Under Italian flag there were several more name changes, until 2004 when she was bought by the Portuguese.

By 2006 renamed the *Athena* and operated by Classic International Cruises, she returned to New York where she sailed from fifty years before on her collision course. Still operating today the *Athena* has recently been arrested and detained several times recently for non-payment of fuel oil bills.

Another outcome of this collision was reported in the <u>American Journal of Psychiatry</u> of November 5, 1957. The article was titled "Some Psychiatric Notes on the *Andrea Doria* Disaster" by Paul Fredman, M.D., and Louis Linn, M.D., who were passengers on Europe bound rescue ship, *Ile de France*. They spent approximately twelve hours independently interviewing and observing the *Andrea Doria* survivors. The article stated in part the following:

> "We were struck by the frequency with which the survivors who spoke to us were angered. They expressed certainty that the accident was the fault of the *Andrea Doria*, even though the details of the catastrophe—such as the extent of the survivors' misery, the irreparable loss of the beautiful ship, the relatively intact state of the *Stockholm*—favored sympathy on behalf of the *Andrea Doria*."

> "Such attitudes are familiar expressions of the quest for a scapegoat, a psychological device for turning aggression outward. It is part of the overall attempt to master an overwhelming trauma. The survivors' tendency to blame the *Andrea Doria* for their misery derived from their feeling of having been failed. They suffered a narcissistic injury which may be compared to the feelings of a child who finds that the strength of his father has turned out to be a fallacy. Let us not forget that the *Andrea Doria* had been considered unsinkable, which conveyed a great sense of security in her passengers; yet there they were having to abandon her and being abandoned by her, experiencing the inability of a parent to cope with disaster."

The facts are that the crew of the *Andrea Doria*, with the expected exceptions, acted with generosity and even heroism. It has been recorded by Cornelius Ryan in an article for <u>Colliers'</u> and by Walter Lord in an article for _Life_ how an Italian cabin-class waiter and several Italian crew members cooperated in trying to free the wife of a passenger from beneath a collapsed partition, spending five hours in the futile effort. Many other instances of helpfulness and altruism on the part of crew members are on record, leaving no basis for condemnation.

Expressions of prejudice were not confined to fixing the blame for the accident on the _Andrea Doria_, but also manifested themselves in the contempt voiced by some passengers on the _Ile de France_ toward Italian immigrant survivors because of their uncontrolled demonstrations of despair. To some who expressed these feelings it was explained that patterns of emotional expression are culturally determined and that they vary, in a given national group, from one economic stratum to another. It was also indicated to them that the control of emotional expression under stress is not a reliable measure of courage and strength of character; furthermore, that from a psychiatric point of view the expression of one's true feelings, particularly during bereavement, serves a useful adaptive function in the mental health of the individual.

Such opinions among _Ile de France_ passengers thus were clearly based on paranoid projections of stereotyped prejudice, in contract to the reactions of the rescued whose resentment toward the _Andrea Doria_ stemmed from the violent destruction of their sense of security and dependence.

The Problem of Communications

The most frequently voiced charges were: that no announcement had been made about the nature and gravity of the accident, and that no concerted rescue effort was made.

> _Comment_ – These have been answered by the fact that the first impact of the collision caused a power failure on the _Andrea Doria_, putting the public address system out of commission. Moreover, the ship rapidly developed a severe list which, coupled with oil slicks on the decks, made it

imperative for each person to save himself from sliding into the sea. These circumstances also made it almost impossible to circulate information on foot. As a matter of fact, Italian crew members did make their way about on the sharply inclined decks, urging passengers to remain calm, and there was indeed very little panic.

A question always asked is: Why did Captain Calamai not speak out in self defense? The only reply to this is another question: How could he defend himself against something for which he had never been charged? There is not the slightest doubt that Captain Calamai was used as the scape goat in this case. In setting him up for this role his owners and lawyers made only a cursory attempt to defend him against the *Stockholm's* perjury. Thus, the case became a matter of Captain Calamai versus, not only the *Stockholm* but also, the *Andrea Doria's* owners and lawyers. Had Captain Calamai done, or even attempted to do, what the *Stockholm* accused him of doing, he should have been charged with criminal intent to cause the collision in which fifty-one persons perished. Thus charged, he would have been able to enlist legal assistance to defend him in the court of proceeding following his indictment. Under these circumstances, the truth of the matter would have come to light. Obviously, neither steamship company nor their attorneys wanted anything like this to happen and were careful to keep the matter under control. It would have been interesting to know how this case would have turned out had the *Andrea Doria* not been caught operating with a calculated risk.

Many have read <u>Collision Course</u>. Consequently there were discussions concerning what Alvin Moscow had written. Those who said they had read the book generally agreed that Moscow had distorted the facts with half truths and innuendos. Facts that would reveal the truth are separated by 200 or more pages to destroy the reader's continuity of thought.

Alvin Moscow was the newspaper reporter who represented the Associated Press at the official inquiry into this tragedy held in New

York City. At the completion of the inquiry, Mr. Moscow obtained nearly a year's leave of absence from the Associated Press in order to devote his full time to writing the book. In producing the book, Mr. Moscow used the copious notes he had accumulated during the long inquiry. He also had full access to the more than 6000 pages of the testimony's transcript. When *The New York Times* published Walter Lord's review of <u>Collision Course</u>, on March 15, 1959, the newspaper wrote that while writing the book, "He (Mr. Moscow) voyaged to Europe on the *Stockholm*, 'interviewing everybody in sight.' He visited the ship's bridge, studied radar, asked officers 'why you did just that?'" It may have been beyond his capabilities to comprehend what the *Stockholm's* officers and the Swedish American Lines fed him but Alvin Moscow changed the testimony and facts.

After traveling through Europe interviewing survivors, Mr. Moscow returned home on a ship of the Italian Line where he interviewed additional survivors. <u>Collision Course</u> is the primary source of reference for this collision and thereby on the cause of the collision. After reading the book, it becomes clear that the fault lies with the *Andrea Doria*.

Pseudo Experts

Both Alvin Moscow and Walter Lord have been described as pseudo experts who write with apparent authority on subjects they have little or no knowledge of. This they do with no respect for the lives and reputations of those involved. The references to Alvin Moscow were contemptuous while, Walter Lord, they indicated, was simply ignorant of the technical and nautical aspects of the sinking of the Titanic.

Some who read <u>Collision Course</u> said they had no recollection of reading anywhere in the book where the *Andrea Doria* executed the "S" turn at a speed in excess of 2,500 miles per hour. This is correct. Mr. Moscow did not spell this out specifically. However, when one studies and plots the third officer's testimony recounted in <u>Collision Course</u>, it becomes crystal clear that the *Andrea Doria* would have been required to execute this maneuver in order to reach the collision from where Mr. Moscow placed her one minute before the accident.

According the to the text of the *Stockholm's* petition, published in *The New York Times*, it was subtlety stated that the *Stockholm had turned away and into the Andrea Doria at the same time*. The third officer's testimony, as outlined in the newspapers and later by Alvin Moscow in <u>Collision Course</u>, told the identical story in greater detail.

In <u>Collision Course</u>, Mr. Moscow has taken this perjured testimony and by manipulation has attempted to create what he claimed is a "factual and true accounting of what happened." He never did divulge who his "maritime admiralty" experts were. Therefore, we must assume they were the bridge officers on the *Stockholm* with whom he consulted while he and Mrs. Moscow journeyed to Europe.

On September 13, 1975, John Carrothers and the author spoke at a conference of naval reserve officers in Norfolk, Virginia. The majority of those attending were merchant marine officers with a keen interest in the *Andrea Doria–Stockholm* case. Also attending the conference was Eugene Underwood, the principal attorney who had represented the *Andrea Doria* at the official inquiry.

Because we believed that Mr. Moscow had been paid to write <u>Collision Course</u>, the book received considerable attention. It was here that Mr. Underwood publicly announced that the Swedish American Line, owners of the *Stockholm*, had paid Alvin Moscow to write the book. He did not go into details other than to say that the *Stockholm's* owners had paid for a trip to Europe for him and his wife while he was writing the book. Thus, our suspicions were confirmed.

Concerning the *Andrea Doria's* course recorder, Mr. Moscow writes on page 291 in <u>Collision Course</u>, "The course recorder graph of the *Andrea Doria*, containing the crux of the controversy on the position of the ships before collision, was more difficult to interpret. Nowhere on the graph was there a clear and definite jog of the pen to indicate the point of collision, such as there was on the *Stockholm's* graph." The *point of collision* shows up on the *Andrea Doria's* graph as clear as a bell, just as it would on any ship's that had been subjected to, as he writes on page 82, "with the force of a battering ram of more than one million tons, the *Stockholm* prow plunged into the speeding Italian ship." The graph clearly shows the *point of collision* when the *Andrea Doria* was on a compass heading of 272°, from which point she was thrust into a long three minute left turn of 92 ° (Mr. Moscow says it was 110°) after which the stricken ship started swinging slowly to her right or damaged side.

Mr. Moscow tells us on page 293, "In that left turn lies the controversy. The *Doria* officers say their ship was struck by the *Stockholm* at about 2310 when the *Doria* had swung only ten or fifteen degrees at the beginning of the hard left turn." He continues in the same paragraph that the *Doria's* officers disputed the Sperry Company's expert witness' interpretation that the *Doria's* graph "shows no indication of collision."

When a difference of opinion, such as this, arises at a Coast Guard or Naval Inquiry the panel resorts to a simple solution. With plots the ships are placed in their claimed headings at the instant of collision. Then the advances and compass headings are worked back minute to a point as far as necessary to determine just how the ships arrived in collision. Figure 6 is what is believed to be the true interpretation of the graphs. Because this is precisely the *Doria's* officers' claim, it is not necessary to produce an identical plot for comparison. Figures 2 and 3 are the interpretation of the same graphs as claimed by the Swedish Line and Charles Haight, their attorney; neither of which agrees with the third officer's testimony.

Mr. Moscow writes that after the lookout had sung out "lights to port", the third officer also saw the lights right where he had expected to see them from his radar plot. He again checked the radar and found the *Andrea Doria* to be 1.8 or 1.9 miles away. Again, Mr. Moscow omits vital testimony and waits exactly 200 pages to finish the third officer's testimony in this respect. On page 255 the full testimony is given

"1.8 to 1.9 miles ahead of him, bearing twenty degrees to the left." In Chapter Two, Mr. Moscow continues that the *Andrea Doria* was showing a weak red left sidelight with masthead lights indicating a safe port side-to-port side passing. He then ordered a two point (22½ °) right turn away from the *Andrea Doria*.

Why does there exist this gap in the reading of his book? Because Alvin Moscow could not reconcile the fact that the *Stockholm* turned away from and into the *Andrea Doria* at the *same* time.

The analysis eventually found its way back to the Naval Institute where it was published in the August 1971 issues of the <u>Proceedings,</u> twelve years after it had originally been submitted by John Carrothers. A copy of this issue of the <u>Proceedings</u>, which exonerated Captain Calamai, was enroute to him in Genoa, Italy, when he passed away.

During the initial official inquiry it became more and more difficult to understand how the *Stockholm's* third officer was able to give, let alone get away with, testimony that was so obviously fabricated. When Captain Calamai's company and lawyers did not defend him against this abuse it became apparent that he was intended to be to the scapegoat in the settlement of this case. Then to top this off Alvin Moscow has perpetuated this infamous story with <u>Collision Course</u>. In reading <u>Collision Course</u> there is an undercurrent of guilt by the *Andrea Doria*. In addition to gaps in the text that misleads the reader there are photos that imply the *Andrea Doria's* guilt. There is a photo of the *Stockholm's* radar that indicated *it had been checked for accuracy the day before.* There is no mention of the lack of a gyro compass input that made determination of true bearings difficult. On a photo of the *Andrea Doria* chartroom it is stated, "the radar plotting device was in the top drawer." What is a radar plotting device? Many of my fellow mariners do not know what this means except to imply an error of omission. The book's last photo is one of Captain Calamai being led away by officials. Again, the implication is "the guilty one" is actually Captain Calamai. By innuendo, omission of facts and fabrication the guilt of the *Andrea*

Doria is implied throughout the book. It may appear that this analysis is a defense of Captain Calamai—such is not the case—it is a defense of what he represents.

The July 24, 1972 issue of <u>Newsweek</u> magazine renewed this infamous story of Captain Calamai. This was due to the occasion of the 16th anniversary of the tragedy when Captain Gunnar Nordenson, Captain of the *Stockholm*, was featured in the Where Are They Now? department of that magazine. Every effort to learn where <u>Newsweek's</u> editors had done the research for this feature ended in frustration. Nevertheless, you can recognize the influence of <u>Collision Course</u>.

The feature quotes Captain Nordenson as saying, "I did my duty. The captain of the *Andrea Doria* couldn't handle the radar and made a last-minute panic turn." The feature also said, ". . . the Swedish American Line showed its confidence in Nordenson the following spring by rewarding him with command of its new flagship, the *Gripsholm* . . ." It continued, "Nordenson lives (in retirement) in a small apartment near the Swedish port city of Gotenborg . . . where he is now 'writing his memoirs."

Captain Calamai was cast off by his employer at the end of the official inquiry. In an obituary notice by *The New York Times*, published on April 10, 1972, John Carrotiers, a marine expert, stated, "the most tragic figure to come out of the disaster is Captain Piero Calamai, master of the *Andrea Doria*. A victim of circumstances, he sat alone, brokenhearted, unable to defend himself . . . of all the principals involved, companies and individuals, Captain Calamai is the least responsible . . ."

Three months to the day, prior to publishing this feature, <u>Newsweek</u> carried the account of Captain Calamai's death in its Transition department. Here it said at the conclusion of his obituary notice, published April 24, 1972, "Friends said he died of crepacuore (broken heart)." His last words before dying were "are the passengers safe?"

Repercussions

The major contributions causing the collision have been addressed through the following.

▶ Aboard passenger vessels today bridge teamwork procedure courses are mandatory. They include proper manning of the bridge when in restricted visibility. This includes the presence of the master on the bridge during such times. The only officer on the bridge of the *Stockholm* was 26-year old Ernst Carstens-Johannsen. Captain Gunnar Nordenson was in his cabin below. Carstens-Johannsen saw no need to call the master to the bridge or he was possibly intimidated by his master who was considered a hard taskmaster of the tightly run *Stockholm*.

▶ In 1956, radar was in its infancy on passenger vessels and there was no requirement for watch officers to demonstrate their proficiency in its use. Range scales are now illuminated so watch officers can easily distinguish which scale is in use. Watch officers must demonstrate their competence in the operation of radar as an aid to prevent collision. This fact must be verified by an endorsement to their license which must be updated every five years.

▶ Inbound and outbound ships are required to use prescribed sea lanes. This is regardless of whether they are within a major port approach area, such as New York, or in constricted waterways, such as the English Channel or the Singapore Straits.

▶ Passenger and cruise ships require two officers be on watch, instead of just one, especially in restricted visibility, in congestive waters, and for arrivals and departures. Masters are now more ready to come to the bridge when called. This relationship between the master and watch officers is vital and emphasized during bridge teamwork courses.

T/S *Andrea Doria*
(Courtesy of Mariner's Museum, Newport News, Va.)

M/S *Stockholm*
(Courtesy of Mariner's Museum, Newport News, Va.)

Crippled bow *Stockholm* minus 75 feet of bow
(Courtesy of Mariner's Museum, Newport News, Va.)

Sinking of the *Andrea Doria*
(Courtesy of Mariner's Museum/Harry Trask)

Captain Harry Gunnar Nordenson and
Third Officer Ernst Carstens - Johannsen of the
Stockholm at the inquiry (Associated Press)

Captain Eugenio Giannini,
3rd Officer of the Watch on the *Andrea Doria*
(Courtesy of Captain Eugenio Giannini)

David Bright presenting a 1st class dinner plate recovered from the *Andrea Doria* to author in 2003

▶ *All* vessels must be equipped with VHF radio sets for bridge-to-bridge (ship-to-ship) radio-telephone communications. This facilitates the exchange of maneuvering intentions between ships.

▶ Global positioning systems have replaced the time consuming radio-direction finder (RDF) and LORAN as navigational aids as a means to fix the ship's position. Thus, more time is devoted to keeping a good lookout, which is the watch officer's primary responsibility.

Conclusion

Case studies, such as this collision, help point out human errors and provide lessons for which every watch officer should profit. Human reaction to such cases generally is one of "that would never happen to me" or "I would never have committed that error." Until you are placed into an identical situation you cannot say for certain whether you would commit the same error.

Safe navigation to avoid accidents can be accomplished with bridge organization through proper prior planning and compliance with the three Cs: communication, coordination and cooperation. It is essential that watch officers support their masters in the safe navigation of their vessels. It is imperative that all watch officers and the master be familiar with all bridge equipment and bridge procedures, and they navigate safely as a team.

Failure to use equipment correctly can be avoided with hands-on training. Correct actions that are intuitive and instinctive in the event of an emergency can be accomplished. The human error problem can be solved with proper training and hands on training both ashore and aboard ship. The most cost-effective method to accomplish this is through simulator training and its use should be greatly increased in the interest of safety at sea.

Presently there are up-to-date lifeboats/life-rafts and lifesaving equipment for passengers and crew. Passengers should assume personal responsibility by reading all safety instructions and knowing two different routes to their fire and abandon ship stations. There is no substitute for taking precautions and being prepared.

With all of the above technological improvements and the right attitude aboard passenger vessels, we can answer 'yes' to Captain Calamai's question, *"Are the Passengers Safe?"*

EXCERPTS FROM RADIO LOG

JULY 25, 1956

Collision time plus:

12 minutes	SS. *Andrea Doria*	SOS – SOS—DE, ICEH.
13 minutes	*Doria*:	Collision with another ship.
13 minutes	M/V *Stockholm*	CQ—CQ—(attention all stations)
		Collided with another ship—message follows.
17 minutes	SS Robert E. Hopkins to *Doria*	
17 minutes	Roger.	Roger.
18 minutes	*Doria* (to Hopkins)	CQ—CQ—0325 GMT Latitude 40-30N,
	Doria	Longitude 69-53W.
21 minutes		My position 69-36W; 40-35N.
22 minutes	SS Cape Ann (to *Stockholm*)	Are you getting assistance; we are about 150
	SS Lionne (to *Doria*)	miles east.
29 minutes		Need immediate medical assistance.
33 minutes	*Doria*	Position 40-28N, 68-56W, do you need assistance?
33 minutes	SS Ile de France (to *Doria*)	Position 40-37N, 69-00W. Standing by.
40 minutes	Hopkins (to *Doria*)	CQ—CQ—SOS—SOS—SOS; position 40-
	Doria	30N, 69-53W; need immediate assistance.
42 minutes		We are 7 miles south of Nantucket and
	USNS Private Wm. H. Thomas	proceeding. (to *Doria*)
42 minutes		Roger.
45 minutes	*Doria* (to Thomas)	Am going to assist—will arrive 0545 GMT, are
	Ile de France (to *Doria*)	you sinking—what assistance to you need—
		signed Captain
52 minutes		8 miles from you—arrive 45 minutes.
52 minutes	Cape Ann (to *Doria*)	Roger.
57 minutes	*Doria* (to Cape Ann)	CQ—CQ; collided with *Andrea Doria* at
	Stockholm	0310 GMT position 40-34N; 69-45W; still
		investigating our damage.
59 minutes		Foggy but can see *Andrea Doria* sometimes.
59 minutes	*Stockholm*	10 miles south of Nantucket proceeding in
	Thomas	dense fog.
1 hour, 11 minutes		Badly damaged, whole bow crushed; #1 hold
	Stockholm (to *Doria*)	filling —have to stay in our position. If you can
		lower lifeboats we can pick you up—you have
		to row to us.
1 hour, 12 minutes		3 miles from you now—have two lifeboats, no
	Capt Ann (to *Doria*)	motorboats.
1 hour, 18 minutes		We are too bending [listing]; impossible to
	Doria (to *Stockholm*)	put lifeboats at sea—please send immediate
		assistance—lifeboats.
1 hour, 19 minutes		Preparing lifeboats.
1 hour, 26 minutes	*Stockholm* (to *Doria*)	Arrived on scene; standing by between ships in
	Cape Ann	collision.

1 hour, 33 minutes	Cape Ann	Lifeboats launched.
1 hour, 34 minutes	Thomas (to *Doria*)	Have you in radar 10 miles; have 8 boats.
1 hour, 49 minutes	*Stockholm*	No boats in water; we are waiting; #1 hold full of water.
1 hour, 52 minutes	Ile de France (to Cape Ann)	Arrive scene 0545 GMT—what can I do to help; several boats ready.
1 hour, 54 minutes	Cape Ann (to Ile de France)	*Doria* says she immediately needs lifeboats for about 1,000 passengers and 500 crew.
1 hour, 56 minutes	*Stockholm*	Heavy damage; about 500 passengers, 200 crew.
1 hour, 58 minutes	*Stockholm* (to *Doria*)	Now launching lifeboats—headed for you.
2 hours, 09 minutes	Thomas	Closing in—have boats ready.
2 hours, 15 minutes	*Doria*	CQ—CQ—danger immediate—need lifeboats— as many as possible—cannot use our lifeboats.
2 hours, 17 minutes	*Stockholm*	Now launching all 12 lifeboats—position Lat. 40-34N; Long. 69-45W—close to *Doria*.
2 hours, 29 minutes	Nantucket Lightship	Weather foggy—visibility 15 yards.
2 hours, 35 minutes	Thomas (to *Doria*)	Two lifeboats on way over now.
2 hours, 36 minutes	*Doria* (to Thomas)	Roger—Tell other ships thousand passengers.
2 hours, 38 minutes	*Doria*	Don't know how long can use radio—I am listing too much.
2 hours, 43 minutes	SS Manaqui	Will arrive 0900 GMT—have 2 lifeboats
2 hours, 43 minutes	Cape Ann	Actuates automatic alarm on 500 kilocycles and rebroadcasts *Andrea Doria's* distress signal and position.
2 hours, 45 minutes	SS Free State	Will arrive 1100 GMT.
2 hours, 51 minutes	Hopkins	Am about 18 miles east—will arrive in one hour— have 4 boats.
3 hours, 02 minutes	SS Tarantia	Will arrive in about 4 hours.
3 hours, 08 minutes	Ile de France	Now have ten boats in water.
3 hours, 11 minutes	Cape Ann	First boat with survivors now on board.
3 hours, 15 minutes	Hopkins	Asks ships in collision if fog is heavy.
3 hours, 16 minutes	*Stockholm* (to Hopkins)	No—not bad.
3 hours, 17 minutes	Thomas (to Hopkins)	Visibility on scene about 3 miles.
3 hours, 23 minutes	*Stockholm* (to Ile de France)	Our foreship damaged--#1 hold flooded— otherwise ship tight—will try to proceed New York slow speed—if you are going there with survivors could we as a precaution keep company?
3 hours, 29 minutes	*Doria*	Need immediate tug assistance.
3 hours, 36 minutes	Ile de France (to *Stockholm*)	Will proceed New York full speed when all rescued—please ask another ship—my schedule imperative.
3 hours, 38 minutes	Cape Ann	Require medical assistance urgently for survivor.
4 hours, 27 minutes	Hopkins (to Ile de France)	Are you handling distress traffic?
4 hours, 27 minutes	Ile de France (to Hopkins)	Affirmative.
4 hours, 28 minutes	Cape Ann	Have about 120 survivors on board—more coming.
4 hours, 30 minutes	Thomas	Have about 50 survivors on board—more coming.
4 hours, 40 minutes	*Stockholm*	Urgent—nearest Coast Guard Station—have 3 serious casualties aboard—need immediate attention—please send helicopter to our position—40-34N—69-46W.

5 hours, 15 minutes	*Stockholm*	Have approximately 425 survivors aboard.
5 hours, 26 minutes	USNS Sgt. J.E. Kelly	Have one doctor aboard ETA one hour.
5 hours, 42 minutes	Manaqui	Arriving distress position now.
5 hours, 47 minutes	Ile de France (to *Stockholm*)	All passengers rescued—proceeding New York full speed—Thomas standing by *Andrea Doria*—no more help needed. Signed-Master.
5 hours, 54 minutes	Cape Ann	Have approximately 175 passenger survivors aboard.
6 hours, 01 minutes	Cape Ann	Proceeding New York.
6 hours, 24 minutes	*Stockholm*	Please—any word of helicopter?
6 hours, 32 minutes	Manaqui (to Thomas)	Request release from scene.
6 hours, 32 minutes	Thomas (to Manaqui)	Release granted.
6 hours, 56 minutes	Thomas	CQ—CQ—plenty ships now—no further assistance needed.
6 hours, 57minutes	Thomas	Present weather—wind 3 MPH—sea slight swell—moderate visibility—3 miles.
7 hours, 27 minutes	Hopkins	Picked up one survivor.
7 hours, 36 minutes	Coast Guard New York	No radio contact with *Andrea Doria* since 1000 GMT—believe off the air.
8 hours, 07 minutes	Cape Ann	Have 168 survivors—2 doctors in attendance—proceeding Ambrose ETA 2100Z.
8 hours, 23 minutes	Coast Guard Cutter	*Andrea Doria* now has 45-degree starboard list—master and 11 of crew believed still aboard.
8 hours, 34 minutes	Coast Guard Cutter	Helicopters arrived at scene.
8 hours, 42 minutes	Ile de France	Have about 730 survivors on board.
8 hours, 53 minutes	Coast Guard Cutter	Helicopter with two patients from *Stockholm* leaving for Nantucket.
9 hours, 04 minutes	Coast Guard Cutter	U.S. Air Force helicopter with 3 patients proceeding Nantucket.
9 hours, 33 minutes	Thomas	CQ—CQ—we have been released—U.S. Coast Guard Cutter Evergreen has now taken command of this distress.
9 hours, 44 minutes	C.G.C. Hornbeam	Picked up 45 crew members and master from *Andrea Doria*.
10 hours, 35 minutes	Thomas	Have 156 survivors on board.
	C.G.C. Evergreen	*Andrea Doria* settling rapidly.
10 hours, 48 minutes	C.G.C. Hornbeam	Escorting *Stockholm* to New York.
	C.G.C. Evergreen	*Andrea Doria* sank in 225 feet of water—position 40-29.4N, 69-50.5W.
10 hours, 49 minutes		
10 hours, 58 minutes	C.G.C. Evergreen	Area cleared.
11 hours, 22 minutes		

The first S.O.S. messages sent simultaneously from the *Andrea Doria* and the *Stockholm* had been picked up by Coast Guard monitoring station on Long Island, putting into action probably the most dramatic and effective sea-rescue operation of our time. The United Fruit Company cargo ship Cape Ann also had picked up the damaged ship's messages and relayed them to other ships, and soon the Cape Ann, the Navy transport Pvt. William H. Thomas and the Tidewater tanker Robert E. Hopkins were all hurrying to our rescue but among them they only had ten lifeboats.

The *Andrea Doria's* list was rapidly increasing, and although help was on the way, the danger was immediate. One hour and five minutes after it was struck, the *Andrea Doria* appealed to the *Stockholm* urgently: *"You are one mile from us. Please, if possible come immediately to pick up our passengers."* Captain Harry Gunner Nordenson of the *Stockholm* radioed the *Andrea Doria*. *"Here badly damaged. The whole bow crushed. No. 1 hold filled with water. Have to stay in our present position. If you can lower your boats, we can pick you up."* A minute later, at 12:21 am., the *Andrea Doria* replied, *"You have to row to us."* And the *Stockholm* radioed back: *"Lower your lifeboats. We can pick you up."* Thirteen minutes went by, and then Calamai sent another desperate appeal: *"We are bending [listing] too much; impossible to put boats over side. Please send lifeboats immediately."* Fortunately, by then, Nordenson had established that his ship would not sink, and he prepared to launch seven lifeboats

When notified of this, the Italian captain radioed back: *"Danger immediate. Need boats to evacuate 1,000 persons and 500 crew. We need boats."* The venerable French liner Ile de France had just left New York with a load of passengers and was heading for France. She was 44 miles away from the scene of the accident when the captain received news of the distress message. The decision of the Ile de France captain, Baron Raoul de Beaudan, to turn his ship back with his many lifeboats was what saved this accident from becoming even a greater disaster. Upon arrival on scene the Ile de France had ten lifeboats ready to lower into the water. These boats were larger and could accommodate more survivors than those from other vessels in the area. All told, there were over 32 lifeboats to ferry over 1,600 survivors to safety in the greatest sea rescue in history.

GLOSSARY

aft. The direction toward the stern of the ship.

astern. Behind, or a backward direction in the line of a vessel's fore-and-aft line. When a   vessel moves backward, it is said to move astern.

ballast. Any weight or weights used to keep the ship from becoming top-heavy or to increase its draft and/or trim.

Bearing. Direction of an object. At sea it is a line of position in relation to an aid to navigation or another vessel. The line of position is expressed in terms of compass direction when viewed from a own ship, ie, object bearing 090° means it is due east of own ship.

boat deck. The deck on which the lifeboats are kept.

bow. The forward part of a ship.

bridge. The location from which a vessel is steered and is speed controlled.

bridge deck. The deck upon which the bridge is located.

bulkhead. A vertical steel partition corresponding to the wall of a room, extending either athwart ship (crosswise) or fore and aft.

buoyancy. The ability to float; the upward force of water pressure, equal to the weight of the displaced liquid.

chart. A map for use at sea by navigators.

crow's nest. An elevated lookout station located forward, usually on the masthead.

davit. Crane arm that when lowered can project over the side of the ship in order to lower or raise boats to or from the water.

dead ahead. Directly ahead on the extension of the ship's fore-and-aft line.

deck. A platform extending horizontally from one side of a ship to the other.

displacement. The weight of water displaced by a floating vessel; thus, a ship's weight in terms of long tons (2,240 pounds equal one long ton).

double-bottom. Compartments at the bottom of the ship between inner and outer bottoms, used for ballast tanks, oil, water, fuel, etc.

draft. The distance from the surface of the water to the ship's keel (how deep the ship is into the water).

engine order telegraph (EOT). Found on bridge and engine room—an indicator from the bridge to the engine room of speed request desired by watch officer or captain, which registers speed request of full, half and slow ahead or astern. Also requests for stop, standby engines (SBE), and finished with engines (FWE).

fathom. A measure of length, equivalent to six linear feet, used for depths of water and lengths of rope or chain.

fog signal. Signal on a ship's whistle when in fog. Whistle is usually on ship's stack. Signal in international waters is one prolonged blast (about six seconds) every two minutes. This signal can be sounded automatically from the bridge.

GPS (Global Positioning System). Modern method of fixing ship's position by satellite (not in use by vessels in 1956).

gyro compass. Compass using a motor driven gyroscope instead of a magnetic needle to point north. It points to the geographic or true north pole instead of the magnetic north pole.

helm. Used as the steering wheel of the ship, it is a tiller or a wheel generally installed in the bridge or wheelhouse to turn the rudder in order to change course during maneuvering and navigation.

hull. The main body of a vessel, including shell plating, framing, decks, and bulkheads.

inclinometer. An instrument for determining ocular inclination, angles, and directions of the visual axes.

in extremis. In grave or extreme circumstances. A situation so perilous that both approaching vessels must change course in order to avoid a collision.

Jacob's ladder. A rope ladder suspended from the side of a vessel and used for boarding.

keel. The chief structural member of a ship that extends longitudinally along the center of its bottom and often projects from the bottom. It is the backbone of the vessel.

knot. Speed at sea (one nautical mile per hour equals one knot).

lightship. A stationary vessel (at anchor), carrying a light used for navigation, serving the same purpose as a lighthouse.

list. An inclination to one side.

lookout. A member of the crew stationed on the bridge or on the crow's nest at the top of one of the masts, usually the forward mast. His duty is to watch visually and audibly for any dangerous objects or for other vessels approaching.

loran. A long-range aid to navigational systems in which position is determined by an analysis involving the time intervals between pulsed signals from two or more pairs of ground stations of known position.

M/V. Motor vessel propelled by diesel engines.

muster station. A place on a ship where passengers or crew must gather in case of emergency, same as abandon ship or fire station.

nautical mile. One minute of latitude, approximately 6076 feet; about one-eighth longer that the statute mile of 5280 feet.

navigational rules. The regulations governing the movement of vessels in relation to one another, generally called steering and sailing rules or the rules of the road.

pilot house. The enclosed deckhouse on the navigating bridge from which a ship is controlled when under way.

piloting. Navigation by use of visible references.

porthole. A round opening in the side of a ship, normally kept weather- and watertight by a transparent glass cover.

port side. The left-hand side of a ship when facing forward. The port side of a ship during darkness is indicated by a red side-light.

RDF (Radio Direction Finder). Audible radio signals by which, when obtaining bearings from RDF stations, navigators can cross two or more bearings in order to fix the vessel's position.

S/S—Steam ship or T/S—turbine ship. Vessel propelled by steam turbine.

seaworthiness. The condition of a ship, its sufficiency in terms of materials, construction, equipment, crew, and outfit for the trade in which it is employed. Any sort of damage to the vessel by which the cargo may suffer may cause it to become not seaworthy.

ship's log. A journal used to record any event that may have occurred on board; there may be, for example, an engine room log, a deck log, etc.

stability. The tendency of a ship to return to its upright position when inclined away from that position.

standby engines (SBE). Indicates to engine room to standby for speed change. Used in fog at sea to alert engineers to standby the throttle for immediate maneuvering.

starboard side. The right hand side of a ship when facing forward. The starboard side of a ship during darkness is indicated by a green side-light.

stem. The forwardmost part of the bow.

stern. The rearmost section of the ship.

watchstanding. The duties performed by an officer who assists the captain in surveillance and data handling.

winch. A machine for lifting and lowering cargo and for other purposes that cannot be handled by manual power; it consists of a drum or a barrel around which a rope or a cable is wound to achieve either a lifting or lowering motion.

windlass. A machine used to hoist the anchor.

yaw. To swing or steer off course.

ABOUT THE AUTHOR

Robert J. Meurn, Master Mariner and Captain, U.S. Naval Reserve(Ret), received his Bachelor of Science in nautical Science from the U.S. Merchant Marine Academy (USMMA), Kings Point NY, and his Master of Arts in Higher Education from George Washington University. He taught at Texas Maritime Academy, was Commandant of Cadets and Executive Officer of the TS Texas Clipper, and was selected as Teacher of the Year in 1978. In 1979, he began his tenure as associate professor at the U.S. Merchant Marine Academy. During 1981, he devised and implemented the first watchstanding course in the United States for cadets utilizing the CAORF simulator. Capt. Meurn also served as Dept. Head, Nautical Science Division and was honored again as Teacher of the Year in 1983 and 2003.

Capt. Meurn has authored four books: *Marine Cargo Operations* (4th edition), *Watchstanding Guide for the Merchant Officer* (3rd edition), *Survival Guide for the Mariner* (2nd edition) and *Anatomy of a Collision* (2018). He was honored by receiving the Dept. of Transportation's Bronze Medal Award and the first ever recipient of the Distinguished Service Medal for his contributions to safety in marine transportation.

He has sailed with U.S. Lines, Farrell Lines, American Export Lines, Moore McCormick Line, Grace Lines and Military Sealift Command/Atlantic, he was an active member of the U.S. Naval Reserve, where his last active duty was as a vice commodore during a convoy exercise in December 1988 in Diego Garcia.

Capt. Meurn is a member of, and has presented papers to, the International Navigation Simulator Lecturers Conference (INSLC) worldwide. He is also a member of the Marine Board, National Research Council's Committee on ship/bridge simulation training. Currently, he is a Professor Emeritus in the Department of Marine Transportation at the U.S. Merchant Marine Academy.

CPSIA information can be obtained
at www.ICGtesting.com
Printed in the USA
FFOW02n1132290618
47213860-50027FF